A STATE OF NATURE

written by
Dillon M. Jepsen

Written by Dillon Jepsen
www.dillonjepsen.com

Edited by Patricia Scott
Cover Art by Jaqueline Kropmanns

Publisher's Note: This is a work of creative non-fiction. Names, characters, places, and incidents are anecdotes from the Author's life.

A STATE OF NATURE/ Dillon Jepsen. -- 1st ed.
ISBN: 9798424234088

If you enjoyed the book, please leave a review online. It is appreciated.

Special thanks to,

My readers, thank you for inspiring me to continue. And of course, thanks to all my friends and family for supporting me.

YOU are HERE to CHANGE the LIVES of EVERYONE.

—A STATE OF NATURE

CONTENTS

CHAPTER ONE

THE REALM OF MUNDANE

The light leads to the world of Spirit. In the immersive light stands the future of self. This is where it all begins, your journey to knowing...

I walk the infinite incline in this dark universe. I speak before I think, because I already knew. I learned who I am. I found who I thought I was. I see myself in a perception that shows the contrary form of both light and darkness, where the focus is on the shadow, and the light is simply refraction. The defined presence and the unknowable, both fully felt in wordless chemistry.

I was not predictable because I did not fear death in the year 2012, or the years following. I did not behave in accordance with safety or the concern for life. I shot the bullet at the floor. I tested death multiple times in my psychosis. I pushed my life to its end countless times and went off-script. I went without happiness in a spiraling freefall of mental dimension. In the depths of mind where the Spirit lives visible to our sight, the soul is fully naked and transparent.

Why is it that we stop before our actions and simply watch them unfold? Sleeping yet participating is life in its mundane extreme. We look for guidance outwardly in every participation we encounter in this the material reality folding over the spiritual.

The world defines our existence. It is the collective realm that we use to solicit new meaning and significance to our living experiences and psychological states. We create metaphors to express the abstracted worlds beyond this one. Here we already know a lot, a lot about pain and suffering...

I test the realm of possibility and convey that I always had the chance in my hands. I wanted to prove that and to display it to people. I expressed genuine free-will in a systemized social landscape. In the year 2012 one evening, in an unkempt apartment that was not mine, I put a cigarette out on the palm of my hand while it was lit. I showed no form of remorse for those actions. My expressionless face meeting the few individuals in the room with me, all of whom were high on pills.

They were looking for a reaction and I had none to give. I was sober and my obsession was breaking through reality. At the time I was 19 years old, and I had something to prove, investigate for myself, and show to others. I was communicating about placebos in that brief period of 2012, showing others that pain is simply a sensation that the mind empowers, in common to other physical and mental states.

On another night I set two water bottles onto a table. One bottle was filled with water, and the other with alcohol. Which one is different? The two bottles were indistinguishable beside each other, both contained clear liquid. The mind offers power by desire and our choices gravitate toward the power of desire. It attracts our immediate attention toward what we consider to be of significance to our awareness. Beyond the simple placebos in life, there was much more I was determined to communicate to others. It was my personal project and a destiny that nobody knows about.

What if our greatest desire were the obsession to master knowledge? What happens if our own guidance came only from the inner self in the personal psychic affairs and from higher knowledge gained through a developed relationship of mysticism?

The supernatural realities exist, awaiting to be excavated. These are other foreign perceptions; the ethereal realms are concealed from the modern presentation of the world system. In the present world, we are dead, not alive in the perspective of which we consider spiritual ambition.

The Indigenous tribe seeks wisdom and insight from the soothsayer. To the people, the intense winds give the signal of an incoming storm for which they must find shelter. To the mystic, the storm is offering the same embrace as sunlight and cool air. Yet the connection comes from distress as opposed to a calm. In the storm people feel alive by fearing death, and a few come alive within with no fear.

The presence of energy can take perceivable form, though, in other instances, it does not. Our soul (psyche) can be guided by the divine into a direction of ascension by aspiring toward new height in our awareness of existence. We are elevated in dimension by decision of the Divine Universe. This is an external teacher that is not another human, but rather an omniscience that exists in a specific perception of Nature which surrounds us. It also exists within our personal awareness and mind.

We are determined to be ready according to the judgment of the Divine Universe. A character nobody has met previously to our present mortality, the deified universe, of its own as a multidimensional being. Are you prepared, or do you just think you are?

In 2019, I had the momentary perspective that only once will one intimately meet God, and upon the immediate connection the person forever knows God as the Divine Universe. I witnessed the being of the Divine Universe seated in the center of its realm. Through my experiences, inward epiphanies came from nothing, and knowledge transpired from my investigations into other psychic dimensions unfamiliar to the world.

The Divine both exists and does not exist as its own sleeping lion that lay in Nirvana. The Divine existing presently between the unmanifest and manifest is an anchor holding steady expectation that foreign existence will anticipate intervention. The phenomenon of God comes alive in the moment when necessary.

The Divine will impart a message upon the eventual fate of another eternity. The Divine informs you of eternal destiny, the role that you came to serve from non-existence into existence. Upon coming to your senses with this realization you will be stunned, paralyzed like a stone statue.

A dormant soul comes alive in living universal reality with personal architecture for the opportunity to shape domestic and foreign landscapes in the expression of personal willpower. The story comes to fruition and unfolds with you as the main protagonist. The spirits which have encountered the Divine the one time now eternally exist with reasoning and a purpose provided by an ultimate divine ruling.

I spent time in communion with God through the human experience in my own periods of intense mental illness. Daunting rushes of added information and insight can lead someone into a state of derangement, especially if perception is deviated in nature beyond one known reality. As mentioned in my previous book, Heaven and supreme reality is a world's distance away from our common perceptions. I study theology as a reflection for the theme in creation. I do not personally maintain a religious lifestyle.

A provocative narrative is written by a universe that behaves as an existence stern and demanding. It contains its own character and form of benevolence and tragedy, with endless space and materializations that decorate the endless space. The divine universe and deified presence emanating of purpose in intelligent Nature is guiding us beyond what is present.

I gaze above reality and think in my mind. My personal outlook settled on an understanding of something that only exists in dreams. I chase extraordinary phenomena with no substantive result yet know it can be imagined and directly experienced subjectively. I have left my body previously, taking a few journeys of my own through astral projection. I become that character and I quit acting.

We forget to remember that this life does end, and it ends before it ever finishes. What a finality to have when you die at an early age with the words glossed over by others and the book is not finished. With or without a cause there is no choice in death. One does not look to death to receive anything but rest. For myself, through my clinical depressive episodes, I wanted to die.

I sought to go where my mind ventured to leave behind suffering. My depression locked me in bed with emotional torment and feelings of hopelessness.

In 2019, after a night of wishing to die, even arranging the matter with the spirit of death, I immediately noticed upon waking the next morning that my right arm was completely limp. This lasted for five minutes until I regained feeling. I slept on it, or I was starting to leave this world. I tend to speculate with different focuses and reason for what could be considered insignificant and unlikely. My mind, being aware of a spiritually guided and personal narrative, has the desire to know the story. My dreams deviated by their nature and were hyper realistic at times. I had ventured with deep introspection into the story of my imagination.

To find God, you must go alone. The guidance comes from within to a realm of the personal imagination. There you find your maker, something you cannot conceive, but were brought to. The face without a name that called you child.

The security of the Divine can only come from the Divine, nothing less can compare. It's the familiarity of an embrace from the literal founding of your existence and the deep and eternal comfort of knowing the answer to why.

It is the revolutionary independence of being put on your feet, to know your master by the face of the universe. You are left with the duty to only love more and enlighten the stars on why they shine.

I was at another pivotal moment in 2019. The day had steadily progressed without hesitation and darkened to night. I walked the streets late in the night because the car was undriveable. People would typically avoid these sorts of circumstances if given the opportunity. I did not have the opportunity. It was taken from me. I was intellectually fixated on other things which were not relevant to the situation.

I began walking back home after the trip to the convenience store. A light rain shower began, my clothing was vulnerable to being drenched within fifteen minutes. However, I was close enough home to not worry. This was my nightly routine, aside from the adventures into the fantasy of my mind.

For several months, I was once again getting lost in the diverse and hypnotic realities of my imagination amid my schizophrenic episodes in disorientating and unique states of consciousness. My will to live a normal life and my insatiable, unhinged imagination both warring together, while the stamina of my heart whimpered through several months.

I was trained by my previous encounters with the Abyss. I knew the bizarre and frantic realities, and that I was best in isolation where I could not damage my material life. This world does not understand insanity and general society creates no room for the questions that lead people to madness.

Where there exists a profound unanswered calling for knowledge and understanding, there is the potential to ascend beyond our sense of traditional reality. If we accounted for the inner questioning of existentialism and returned our attention to the world of spirit, then superficial life would be doomed.

We end up asking questions like why we suffer, where are we going, when will this all end, and does it ever. Life is situated in a drought of meaning and purpose. People exchange their livelihoods for security in the material system, accompanied with deceptive delusions of the present. "This is good, this is bad." A disconnect encased in the call for judgment. We have little relationship with supreme existence, so how would anyone know any better?

The world struggles with connection and empathy. The darkest days are characterized by marks of unhealable tragedy. People are often defeated by the inability to make sense of their lives. In society, we perpetuate the expectation to enhance quality of life and provide for the world system. The burden is on the people. The only glam in an obedient life is watching TV sitcoms, relishing in popular culture, and seeking enjoyment from new experiences when possible.

What exists beyond life other than a scenario and our hope to create a positive future? I am glad to expand upon that in this second book. For reference, my first book is titled A State of Mind. Many reflections will be provided for you to balance with your own unique appreciation and perspective.

The journey of the shared experience involves oneself and the others. There is purpose, if it is meaningful to one and another, and vice versa as the mutual balance. Unlike the others, you are ready. People who consciously think upon the deeper mysteries offered by this universe are the minority.

You are in search of the final realization that enables you to separate illusion from the Heavens existing in suspension. If one has set time aside to better understand the self as an intellectual sentience, they are ready. While the capable mind allows one to achieve and the courageous heart pushing one to grow, there is the moment of seeking fulfillment from something that may be simply framed as otherworldly...

We live in a wild universe that offers many directions towards pleasure. We are not defined by the moment or an instance of speculation. We are known by our character and decisions. In the United States, we enjoy entertainment and fine beverages. Or other times we simply want a cheap drink with high liquor content that is easily obtained from the corner store. Life is often known for heights of experience and the readily available awe occurring when we space out and reflect on our existence.

I went through twenty-eight years of being told, or at least having myself convinced, I am wrong for thinking as if I knew anything. Holding onto insecurity and lashing out in spite, I eventually had the tough realization that I had only my own self-assurance in believing the things I thought. I like to see myself as humble and I would like to say that the people all around me like me. This is where I am now?

It can be said that it is easy to be different. You just develop a complex that enables you to willfully object to common beliefs and emphasize distinctive differences between yourself and the world. This book is not aiming to do this, nor attempting to reject common beliefs or magnify the personality. I hope this book is of greater allegiance to the supreme reality and not simply another worldview.

The system we live in on Earth is a world system. It is the description to our reality that provides the context by which we maintain and continue daily lives in an evolving and changing world. We roleplay an identity and are raised to preserve tradition and our heritage. We enter our homes and think little of the world because we want the safe space far away from tragedy and the inevitable.

I am distraught. I am a skeptic to the fact I am distraught. I cannot believe my feelings as they happen in a dance of passion and in nature are as simple-minded as how I feel when I experience ecstasy in the evaporation of self and stress. The feelings happen with climax but pour out like a cloud showering water over the Earth. Happiness, sadness, amazement.. sometimes it can be a little more complicated. It is the belief we are alone that keep us separated. We are alone in the universe, what a delusion.

You can carry your feelings into the next life as you disengage from this life, but you will not take this life, as it must be left. Whether or not your present-day issues are ever resolved, you will leave your life as it is. In preparation of the moment in which we depart this world, we must know what we are leaving behind. Why are we born on Earth? The answer is existential.

We are to serve an objective purpose in a meaningful sphere of life we create. Like mechanical gears in an invention turning and clicking, there is an objective purpose to evolution and to the levels of reality which function to put together the processes of life and creation, for example, the photosynthesis of our spirit through sustenance provided by our inherent attraction to life-giving properties and knowledge-increasing endeavors.

We are to intellectually ascend and master our human nature. We are developing a spiritual relationship to the supernal universe, the celestial existence – one of an ascended state and transcendental nature. The evolved state of connection that is inclusionary to the creative heaven and the kingdom of God.

As we are creatures of the universe, we are mediums to the energies that persist in existence. We are fallible to the lingering deceptions, yet strong in our confidence. We are easily molded by the experiences of Nature which offer resolution to our hunger for engagement. We are attached to the physical plane, glued together by the incessant desire to know more, and give up less.

The phenomenon of Spirit is not unique to humans, nor to other living creations in complement to animistic worldviews. This would directly mean even the universe has a spirit of its own. Seeking to understand more, we want to know where it is all going. What is the final picture of evolution in our grand universe?

We just want to discover the entertainment existing in the universe. Our immediate concern is to have entertainment and our basic needs met. For those seeking otherwise, the grandeur of the evolving, mystical universe is something that mirrors the deep introspections of the inner self. It softens the problems of today and pulls us into tomorrow.

One may encounter trials in the self as consciousness navigates between taught worldly desires and something fonder to the soul. We are often fighting the devils created by this world, not simply ourselves. Some people look at this world and it just makes them angry. I can be one of those people, as I have struggled with emotions like anger or resent I momentarily develop against others. Our attention is focused on an agenda of material gain and not witnessing the universe in humility.

The areas in the world with light pollution do not watch the Milky Way galaxy like areas without. I live in a town where truly little of outer space becomes available at night. It is shut out by society, another telling sign that we sustain an ignorance. We block out what is declared as inconsequential. If something does not threaten, it is discarded as insignificant. The world is without oxygen, and breathing without air appears to be the only choice in the impossible.

We are used to a mundane reality, where everything sits in relationship to other parts of everything. There is a lot one can learn and many things to achieve. However, we are unaware of what kind of seat we have property over in the great hallway of time. The path of progression, the journey to complete resolution, is fundamental in the universe. The identity and perceptions of humankind shaped the present world system. The system is inept to the excellence that is necessary to be demonstrated about the utopian dream of people coming together.

The world is sufficient for serving the needs of a person if they are willing to sacrifice. They will tell you everything is fine, to remain passive. It is difficult to follow the insignificance of dwelling in inaction while remaining in a dying collective that cannot tame personal willpower other than by means of control and deception. Collective existence is strained by a lack of sight for the journey into the Abyss. The Abyss serves not only as a realm for imagination, but as a bottomless suspension of infinite potential, possibility, and unawakened significance. These features are reminiscent to the universe.

The infinite expression of possibility existing within determined parameters is evidence of universal consciousness. The will and intention present in the determinism of the divine universe are characteristic to sentience. This is a speculation that justifies observations between purpose and the present. The agenda which may be perceived within creation is evidence of a deified universe with personality and ambitions. All of this is only witnessed by the choice to engage in an alternative perception. To fray away from the discourse of the troubled world and reawaken what brings life to the mute universe.

The universe is advancing while unraveling as an expanding conception of unimaginable possibility. The unimaginable, or the unmanifest, is the vacant but present manifestation of existence which has not been yet observed or measured. I discussed this in terms of Kabbalah in my initial book, A State of Mind. These ideas are dynamic and fit a million scenarios to help us understand potential and give space for imagination. This opens the space necessary to create.

To express any culture, live any life, and thrive in all ways, is not something the modern world embraces quite yet. The cold descriptive framework of our collective reality lacks color and significance. It is hardened by the pain in the heart, the following numb felt after traumatic repercussions.

A life given to us without cost but the meaning of it is withheld by the Creator. It is by realization of this we transcend the limited and futile worldviews that keep us frozen. When we realize the greater circumstance, it lessens the anxiety when deciding how to behave uniformly in response. We allot more time for calculated efforts and bear the responsibility appropriately. There is a backstory that is set apart from this life, as it is the former existence holding greater authenticity. We are to invest effort into rediscovery of the former.

This world we live in will not reach this magnitude of patience until our species awakens from beyond our sickened existential condition. The world is climaxing, and the consequences will leave us emptier than before. The insecurity brought upon us over time will promote the search for meaning in life.

The beautiful and immersive gaze of our universe pacifies the anxiousness that resides within us. Feeling anxiety from the desire to make haste in response to an intensity of emotions will cease. Our souls prosper in tranquility and feeling as if without limitations. The failure of religious institutions will influence humankind to revisit the ancient spiritual perceptions that guided us before in prehistory.

. . .

At this moment, I would like to formally introduce Mark. Mark as a character in the first book, provided a theme that highlighted the book and its message. There exists more to us and to the universe than we initially suspect.

The universe is alive though seemingly inanimate. The universe contains character in both personification and quality, we are extensions of this image. Mark is an alter-ego in my own depth of awakening personality and character.

In his room, Mark was laying down on his bed. Appearing at the door was a nature spirit. It looked like a blue bird with a long beak, like a blue jay. The spirit wanted to see from Mark's perspective, and so Mark allowed the spirit to enter his body. In Mark's vision materialized two bright blue eyes which he could see in his field of vision. The blue eyes looked around in interest. Mark was carefully introducing the spirit to the experience. The spirit was good natured with a cute appeal and personality.

The spirit, after some time, exited Mark and made company with him. Then in a following moment the spirit shapeshifted from a bird to becoming a tall man with dark features. The man sat down and wrote studiously in a journal placed on the desk in the room. After the morning had passed by, the spirit left and did not return.

We visit things in mind each day as we ponder the thoughts others have pondered before us. When will we be visited by the things in our mind? When will we become the thoughts of others? In our passage beyond death, we become timeless and displaced out of existence into another one. Something of an existence that I say is former to this reality and life, the land of imagination, the realm of thought – the speculative existence.

As living beings that coexist in the material and nonphysical realms of existence part in both reality and mind, we capture the moments we seek in an individual and collective experience. The faint mystical understandings that have not perplexed our minds for over a century, the previous perceptions of reality that gave causation to our past ascensions in individual and group consciousness.

Recall that at the beginning in life, you are blindly discovering the world and universe. We begin without direction, and it is essential to enamor the experience and participate with both willpower and aspiration. Existence must be embraced or it is disengaged. As a child we learn to adapt to the world and life, that is the project. Collective society is centered on inventions of economics and social sciences. It is not us that adapt, what adapts is our ability to manipulate and gain from our circumstances. This does not enable us to succeed in the way that past lived experiences do as we learn from the environment and others. Where this world goes, we may never want to go back.

In my personal life, I am diagnosed with schizoaffective disorder. The disorder is both schizophrenia and a mood disorder. I experience mania, hallucinations, delusions, psychosis, and other symptoms when unmedicated. In my unique and diverse experiences with schizophrenia and fantasy Mark has appeared as a part of myself. I will involve Mark in the narration of my personal life experiences and to add the character for the book. Mark is another part of me that I can only express as my dormant soul coming alive.

Mark has revealed unto myself that there are character qualities of mine which exist and were previously undiscovered. These were existing unknown to myself as a lurking identity that had no stimulation previously until my rapid descension into psychotic states, profound enough to rapture my attention into other creative and supernatural realities. This insight had taught me of a cosmic narrative that exists, one that this world does not know.

The life freely offered to us is lined with the decorations of obvious appeal and hidden purpose. This pushes us to have new experiences and ponder on our individual and collective existence, looking to parallels to see dimension to the descriptive reality we know.

The narrative we understand concerns our societies and cultures. The cosmic narrative is grander as it involves elements of scenario for which we lack awareness. Namely, the creative features that hold significance in our lives like our inherent spiritual capacity for connection with the supreme reality. We can experience an extrasensory connection with our existence, though to do so we must believe in the connection.

As it is never relevant for people to go about lengthy periods of deep reflection or befriend the inner nature of themselves, many never breathe life into their imagination. We are boundless to experience life in the universe. World peace and galactic exploration are completely possible and feasible scenarios. Yes, humankind can and will get to that point – if not be destroyed by the perils of deception and corruption.

Sin has been a common theme in human history, so its speculation is well understood by many who become witness. It is not something many people disagree on, concerning the capacity for some individuals to become corrupted seeking power and behaving without mercy. It is a strange and unfortunate quality about us and our decedents.

I decided on the name Mark in 2014 in just one fleeting moment while sitting on the couch in the living room. This was in effort to embrace and better understand the inner nature that I had discovered in myself, the inner character. What is the narrative that this world does not know presently?

Let us start off by putting the presently accepted narrative into perspective. We live in a world of political affairs, culture, and desperation. We build upon governments that each apply different philosophies and employ various developments of policy. Generations have faced hardships, genocide, persecution, or had the privilege to prosper in a more secure region in the world. Human compassion is considered a charade in cultures where persecution and contempt prevail.

The personal affairs we focus on in our lives tend to be focused on mundane aspects of our reality. There is no present connection to allow a heightened awareness for this world and all parts of existence. Namely, this world exists with a firm veil which separates and creates conditions for the unknown which we build upon with our understandings of the real world.

The veil disguises the true and authentic perceptions of reality that our minds never venture beyond. It holds us to our mental realm of possibility in the limited consideration of only the minor circumstances in this world. The veil exists as lack of perception for the unseen forces. Therefore, without intuitive and guided willpower, the mind never considers the otherworldly.

In this understanding, could we speculate that we are never shaped by anything other than the insignificant differences we are present with? The differences we provoke in conflict will continue to excite further suffering. The pressing matters of climate change, global political dysfunction, and other threats can only be ignored for so long. Correcting our negligence of kindness is more important than mundane issues we heavily invest in.

We are at odds with aggression and haste because there is nothing keeping us alive in this world. We look at each other within the world and see separation. If we looked beyond, there is only connection between us in the universe. The world is straying and volatile. Warmongering and hate politics will throw this world into another period of darkness. The decency in the world is slipping away. Simply put, the mundane world is dying, quickly...

He became articulate with his words, more so than before. He was more daring with his actions, less submissive than before. Mark was slowly individualized by his newfound willpower, and the result was that he was more conscious than before. He sought the necessary moments to learn and understand. The mind equipped with selfless reflection is a tool necessary for growth. In both existence and our inner mind, the universe is a projection of the higher divine, a space within the light.

The universe has a depth of character and personality. I will continue this point throughout this book. A key necessity in the perceptions I discuss is to view the universe as its own living being, as the center of life and evolution. We are alive in Spirit, why would the universe be dead? Everything is alive in Spirit.

Every night we sleep the brain entertains us by vivid and spectacular dreams. In the dreams we can fly, shapeshift, do magic, and much more. Our brains entertain a different type of existence, a former one native to creation. Similarly, how we have a choice to speak or not, the universe has the choice to express or not. Our consciousness is the place of our awareness seated in the mind. The greater existence in speculation is based upon the creative imagination and the narrative is shaped by the pursuit of knowledge. Higher realms are expressed by elevating your awareness and creating distance between yourself and this world.

The creative imagination is nonphysical reality linked to real-world perceptions of our shared physical reality. The alignment of two different horizons coming together in mental dimension allows for a relationship to form. An awakened reality involves the affairs that exist beyond the levels of human interaction and an engagement of understanding the underlying events and causes which lead the people. Two levels of inspiration exist: one centered at the heights of imagination, and one directly involved with reality.

We bring enlightened knowledge from above our sphere of awareness and carry it from the sky to the earthly dominion for others to learn. Humans met gods in bizarre dreams that mimic the phenomenon we understand by astral projection. Alive in our visions the gods gave instruction to humanity in prehistory. The event of encountering entities in the extraordinary states of consciousness is not unusual.

Withholding constant engagement to this reality creates space for other realities to grow and prosper within you. The imagination can perceive information and significance expressed in symbolisms crafted by the unconscious part of mind. The subconscious mind offers unique perceptions created by the mystical language of our inner nature. The concealed yet omnipresent knowledge is communicated by abstractions like a coded book of hidden intelligence, an obscure messaging from a deeper connection that has not been made public by popular conception.

These walls have stories, and these floors carry stains. The once dense and thriving rainforest having been deforested is now starting over. Time is cyclical, a metaphysical parallel to the 360 degrees we observe in geometry. It's a repetitious, audacious, and glowing universe on fire. Forest wildfires happen naturally, the trees leave seedlings to restart their growth after being burned.

In archetypal significance this may allude to Samsara, or the nature of the repeated, opportunistic universe known to recreate itself with the intention of creating surviving conditions for the human creation and general evolution. What occurs if humanity is wiped out into extinction? We would look to find out and then we would find out. It may be different; it may be of the same nature – but we cannot allow our cycles of generational history to be defeated through persistent man-driven cataclysms.

At what great magnitude are we to surmount to? A curiosity in science is being born, will it be neglected in its infancy? We are a phenomenon we know as consciousness in the universe, and we study the phenomena surrounding us and the cosmos.

Human nature can come shy of perfection in idealism but is prone to error and confusion. In a world of individuality when we do not meet the status quo, we are treated with rejection. The world system makes us outsiders in our home. The inner nature and connection to supreme reality strengthens your foundation and emphasizes true individuality in a manner not seen by this world.

You are beautiful and mysterious. You have potential that is embraced. The sense of belonging in the universe does not stem from only our comfort in existence. We feel belonging because the universe also desires our love and potential, so we feel purpose. The world system handicaps us by putting us into roles, in effort to build and create an organized society. You are more than a part in this world system, you are the light that makes it mundane.

The impact that humanity could have within this universe is of great desire to the greater will of the very much alive universe, which acts on its own schematics in progression. As excellence comes to be delivered by the universe, we can reach that standard. In a future when we have survived growing pains as a world, we will be highly focused on achievement and the pursuit of knowledge. We express the same nature as the universe because we were created from the birth of the universe.

At great heights of welfare in the world could the people really focus on discovering every aspect of nature and ponder on what remains hidden. The regressive politics of those who do not believe in the general welfare of the people will continue to stifle the world until a balance is achieved.

As our collective consciousness continues to mature and reform through stages of development, we will experience new states of existence. The next era will be postmodern, an era without religion. This is difficult to see in the present moment because our livelihood and ideologies have been shaped by the church and institutions of religion.

Religion is a social construction developed over time and disseminated by colonialism, prior to that there was no objectification of spiritual worldviews. Spirituality in history was shaped by the relationship between the people among themselves and the creative imagination as the descriptive reality for existence. This was the unevolved basis for contemporary religion.

I struggled with knowing that I was having episodes of the schizoaffective disorder, as I knew the best thing I could do was stay in my room in isolation. My mind was loose on a spree of hallucinations, delusions, and mania. I was captured in the many fantasies created by my imagination, which had a life of its own. My imagination entombed me in my own personal and separate universe joined with mystery and appeal which made it very captivating.

All of this involved myself as a character and revolved around my mental and spiritual maturation and development. I was investigating my reality through personal experience with only myself to be concerned with. In moments, my awareness would be raptured by variable instantaneous manifestations of my subconscious dialogue and imagination.

These manifestations taking shape in auditory and visual forms emanating from inner worlds accessible by mind. The narrative was shaped by conversations, held by the attention of my introspections, whether with myself or with any character of my perceived imagination.

The heightened state of perception caused by my disorder also had a profound impact on the nature of my dreaming states. I had events where I would lay down to sleep and wake up in what felt like a moment but was several hours later. I experienced hyper realistic dreams in which I engaged the same narratives that I was involved in while awake.

My relationships with angels, archangels, deities, and decedents from human history were always significant. These interactions transpired within my own imagination. The narrative was not always accurate in terms of real-world factuality and instead was influenced by my personal chosen perceptions.

The irrational nature of the experiences may reduce them to be insignificant in the opinion of practical-rational thinkers. Though, the personal lived experiences on my behalf have taught me that a lot existing within can come alive with personality. In hallucinations, the imagination within your mind extends into projections of reality. The reaction of entertaining a thought could very well cause a responding event in the perceived imagination and reality. Non-physical reality is thought responsive which infers it is a mental manifestation.

It is all just nonsense, so I should turn away. Do I really think that? Not exactly, and the following is my reasoning. I would be turning my back on my limitless and creative imagination, which I could simply choose real life over. I would argue there is a place for the imagination, though it may not be in this world. It may take place in the world, but on a different layer of meaning of which we point to and perceive.

The global narrative will foster a relationship with non-ordinary existence as generations come to experience phenomena with better understanding. After death is the more relevant situation in which you would enter the creative imagination. And at that point, you are a myth like all the other characters of your mind.

Schizoaffective disorder has brought me a lot of insight on the nature of non-physical reality. It helped establish the medium through which I gained a connection with higher existence. I was forced to face an explosive creative imagination, as if I were a child and daydreaming once again in my life, yet vividly seeing my imagination extend into my perceived reality. My life operated in stories that progressed through several weeks of the months I was unstable.

The narrative was centered on my personal evolution as I was the focus of all the characters in my imagination. In experiencing the alternate realities that lay within the gaps of existences, you evolve into a character of your own making—your own alternative self and persona. This character of the self comes as a reaction to the context of the creative imagination and fantasy. We are presently who we are as being shaped by the world, beyond that is our true character in Spirit.

This book discusses the story of what exists beneath the narrative we live by in this world system. This book is here to help you develop the imagination necessary to navigate your understanding in relationship to the imagination. I named my alternative self as Mark; he is my persona as shaped by the supernatural existences that lay dormant and absent from present awareness.

How do you perceive yourself as the character of your mind? It is by curiosity that you discover the inner self, and it is by affirmation that you are pushed to define it. Mark is meek, he is courageous, he is fearless, and he looks 24 years old if wearing his beard. What am I saying? This is another side of me, not relevant to the world as it exists today, but it is a shade of myself in the Nature that lies hidden.

I have perceived Mark to be within myself, and as a character, he is my alternative self that is folded in the dimension of personal representation. Demons, well, I do believe in them. I have encountered evil entities in my astral projections. The true self in myself manifests as Mark comes alive when sensing demonic presences. I become predatorial and seek to confront the demon immediately to overcome it, whereas a lot of people would become frozen with fear.

Personally, I have no idea why I have this aspect about myself, but it is there, and it is a reoccurring personality trait that comes to be expressed in an otherworldly dimension. Mark clearly knows no boundary and is not likely to fall into fear when facing adversity of the spirit world. I want you to think of yourself with this book, not about me. I reflect personal potential that is all – we all share the same potential and I hope you realize yours along with what makes you a unique part of this literary universe and its cosmic drama.

CHAPTER TWO

MANIFEST DESTINY

Something existed once before as a predecessor to the imagination. Upon the self-awareness of existence came the void, the divisional non-existence. The space from what was became absent and then together everything was drawn into the gap of separation.

From it was created an infinite, more possibility unraveling in a cosmic perception that exists in scientific expressions deducing the imagination that existed once before into a state of Nature.

The stairway into Heaven and beyond to Nirvana begins at the emergence of divine existence then ends with non-existence. It is a rough acknowledgement in understanding to prepare for a never-ending death. Everyone faces that fear when they die. Those who know, they will know, and those who do not, they would have never known without desire. That is the precedent, the urge to discover and know further.

The lack of journey is stumbling towards the door while going inward. Drunken and indeliberate by our emotions and becoming disheartened and disempowered by the brutalities in this world and life.

The collective conventions and connection of all individual thought patterns and systems creating new perception for the meaning of life. The many different shades of human interaction creating many cultural landscapes.

The color of expression and choice of action, both impacting an energetic cosmos to a new form of being and imparted significance. Our inner realm of perception is the source of the energetic power we feel in the landscapes. It's the medium which our consciousness adapts to. We morph into new existences of different circumstance; we are spiritual beings that are evolving to conquer the known universe and all to be desired.

There is no initial beginning yet there is a birth of our dreams. What came before this

Universe? Another universe. We seek information on *God* ... a force that has ruptured the dead universe and gave bursting life once more. We find ourselves in an undead universe, once again breathing. The anterior passive universe *Alpha* came previously. We are in the posterior active universe *Omega*, the reawakening universe emerging from catacombs from the illusion of eternal death. We are overcoming amnesia, learning all over to thrive and to defeat suffering.

An advanced mythology awaits, involving a complex new evolution of God containing more archetypes. God is the *Alpha* and *Omega*, the beginning and end. These are stages of eternity and reincarnation – the expression of not, and the death and rebirth.

I had sought out at the age of eighteen to experience an *ego-death*. I had read previously about it and developed my own understanding of it. I wanted to have the experience; I do not think I knew why back then. I had gone to church being told to think a certain way. That is why I wanted to experience something that 'supposedly' could bring insight. I remember being curious about psychedelic states.

I had an insatiable desire to investigate into more concerning the nature of reality and its metaphysics. I wanted *experiential* evidence so to begin postulating what I personally thought about this world and universe. I did not need drugs or religion to help me find these answers as I was called into the next year. 2012, the year which wiped the slate clean with showering realizations that proved nothing about this reality is simple.

The days of that former understanding of life were numbered and came to an upset and defeat. Developing Schizoaffective disorder at 19 years old was my 'signed contract' to a year of ego-death. I thought that I were a *no-name*, somebody without a name.

No identity, no rights, no willpower. I lost my name and consequently lost my soul. That was my entrance into that year, losing my identity. I found a new willpower from the death of my old life. In mystical states of consciousness seeing reality in a distinctive perception I can only explain as *apocalyptic*.

At the stopping of time, the impossible becomes possible. The walls around the house fall to reveal what is outside, the watching eyes in the field, the patient owl in the tree, and the angels in the streets. The dimension above time descends to fill the space where time ceases. The curtains are pulled away and the hidden forces of reality are revealed. Everything becomes subjective and there is nothing but phenomenon. The clock breaks away and you are standing before an eternity.

The best thing you can do with your life is learn how to be gentle with all matters including your words, love, and actions. If we strive to meet the basic qualities of goodness we can attain the demeanor that makes us pure. To recall childhood is to be reminded of a former youth you have deviated from. All bad people can become good, a lot of good people end up becoming bad.

We have a feature to ourselves that holds our allegiances. What do we defend and protect as our foundation? Surely, if we do not guard our foundation, it will be devastated by what we allow into our hearts and lives. As creatures created from a meaningful existence, we need *something* to belong to. We belong to what was once before, we began at the beginning, and that was prior to now and before the then that is...

Why look at the universe in fantastical perceptions with renewed and evolving significance? This creates the inspiration for new perspectives and heightened perceptions to enter your mind. The creative imagination sustains youth and helps define the internal significance of collective existence. Without sight for this, your soul will not move.

Your vision for the otherworldly cannot be influenced by worldly perceptions because such has no place in higher states of existence. The errors of our own, the mistakes that follow, are in consequence no part of the higher whole that we descend from as human beings. The aspiration for grand intelligence is a state of perfection. As spirits with human intelligence and form we are with attributes of the mystical phenomenon present in the universe. We hold relationship with the divine universe by the simple question of a unique connection that we encounter and surface in awareness.

Everything is a simple perception of the physical. At further thought, the physical matter is motivated by energy, then the forces are mystical agents at the determination of further unforeseen influence designing an intelligent environment with us as actors. From the mystic in ourselves we hold psychic relationship with the greater hierarchy of existence. It is a connection.

Manifest a psychic acuity for the spirit of nature by maintaining a passive attention for the lively Nature of your environment. What do the trees hold in quality, what do the ancient landscapes know? What may you sense from your peers? The energetic temperament of the universe? The universe tells us to be patient and aware. The universe incorporates a story to learn and visions to witness, to keep us alive in spirit with anticipation fueled by aspiration and hope. When will you witness the literary narrative of our universe and not simply the one in this world?

With our present complex, we do not behave as if we are in mystical relationship with the living personified universe. We act independently. We found the ability to measure our world and put it into terms we could create order with. Therefore, the dependent relationship with the deified universe is not exactly like it was in prehistory.

In prehistory, animism was foundational in cultural and spiritual worldviews. A relationship with the spirit reality functions with an extra sense of knowing and perception. It is a private engagement with existence, no less. You are in an intimate and personal shared existence with the planet and the stars above. This consistent understanding is muffled by the attention instead being consumed in daily life focusing on maintaining security and contentment. If we were a little freer, we could live in a world of our own making.

The providence of Heaven starts at a stairway that begins from this world. We are downstairs, away from an awake, aware, and living Heaven, and we dwell in a lack of recognition for this. The universe is alive when we are alone, it gives company in solitude. The inner heaven is a creative paradise in a realm shaped by the private introversion of the soul, and it flourishes and grows with an active and inspired imagination.

A post-apocalyptic reality.. a circumstantial change following an order of unsuspecting events. The condition is the future, and the veil has been lifted. The veil keeping other dimensions hidden, that of which exists beyond the present time, has been broken by a new dawn of clairvoyance and understanding. What we were ignorant of, we could no longer ignore. The afterlife will merge with this world upon the *unveiling*, the Apocalypse. The mystery and unknown, raptured away from the sleeping populations as the collective encounter presence of the formerly unmeasured existence of the otherworldly.

The identity never faded, the only ending to the universe is when the universe shuts you out. It is either embrace your livelihood in this challenging time or fall to the pursuit of revenge against the forces that abandoned the light with ease. A spirit that recognizes the dismissal of Spirit becomes reactionary. The Spirit is a flame that humanity has never allowed to slip away. This calling of the divine light is what will lead the future of human generations, and that same light will be the center of the collective spirit in the people. It comes with no price, is sacred, and exists beyond the reach of sin and lesser deceptions therefore is undeniable.

The imagination is the breath of the soul. If the imagination has died, then the soul is withering away. Just prior to death, we no longer can imagine a future in this world. We can only think of what is beyond and make peace with it, in the hope it loves us and accepts our dying spirit. The return to unified consciousness is the realm of spiritual existence. The projections of this existence is ripping through the dead universe and raising life from the lifeless.

The reincarnation of the universe, the meeting and conjunction of two known divisions of existence, the dead and alive. The unknown and known, coming together in congruency by epiphany and realization. The mystery succumbs in the presence of knowledge. The heights of the imagination are descended in perspective by the predisposition of nihilism. If you do not have a world existing within and therefore the external world is meaningless and calls for no pursuit, then what are you going to turn to when you have fallen weakened?

We begin to reach inside when there is nothing left for us to touch or feel, we turn inwards in reaction. The absent-minded realities that we frequent so often are the graves we never leave upon death. We lay there and die, later to be exhumed by Hades and released as a passenger heading towards purgatory. If there is no definition to what exists beyond, you will enter the next world clueless and confused. We are deceased upon the physical end; we are only survived by the spirit and unraveling curiosity of what exists beyond the blanket of darkness.

. . .

Mark was sitting in the room during the afterhours of the environment. Sitting in different chairs in the room were two deities from the Egyptian pantheon. The three of them were looking toward and away from each other in perpetual trance. They moved through the passage of the Du'at, the Egyptian halls of the afterlife. The three remained attentive as they transitioned together through a series of subliminal and psychic transmigratory transfers of consciousness, through doorways leading to deeper reality from waking state consciousness, toward the destination of delta-wave existence.

Like being the passengers seated in a boat, wading through the rivers while blinded by an ominous darkness and lacking awareness, meanwhile following the intuitive held within. Those who lost their focus amid the traveling of transmigration are left behind in the wake of the boat, severed from the rest of the group.

The afterlife is a strange and empty existence only understood by an awakened intuitive. To be lacking an informed spiritual intuitive may easily disturb an individual leading them to become lost. By enhancing your acuity on situation, you understand the underlying sub-context and behave appropriately. This can be of much use when traveling through unfamiliar worlds.

Learning the authentic nature of the universe helps you understand possibilities.

Supreme reality always is accessible by our reception of higher reality. The higher realm exists within the imagination as an accessible part of our perception when your self is allowed to be familiar with conceiving otherworldly realities. To be able to involve your meditations with the personal and aspiring universe is a technique that needs practice and consistent engagement. The relationship between your mind and the creative source of the inspired universe is shaped to be personal in your imagination.

It is through this *sense* and relationship with supreme reality that your intuition is informed. Finalizing the self in your imagination may establish new lucidity within your personal psyche. It is beginning to look from within with the knowledge already internalized to guide your thought process. Imagination is developing internal awareness for personal microcosms of pensive and exploratory purpose. In better understanding the world within you help yourself justify existence in the outside world. The universe is in a collective pursuit of personal inquiry for knowledge, the objective of God.

Jewish mysticism created a system that combines features of conscious and metaphysical projection into a system of perception known as the Tree of Life. With its unique intersections and studies, it reveals relationship between the different forces of Nature. The origination of existence is from light that extends into the surrounding visible universe. The wellspring of all creation is a massive *all-natural* singularity that exists within the depth of reality. The singularity is something I term as *source* as it is the source of all creation. The characteristic of 'all-natural' meaning an organic and pure form of evolving intelligence working in Nature.

The passage of *Ohr*, a Kabbalist term for light, participates in all emanations of reality. If an individual reasons in meditation holding connection with light and perspective of supreme reality in mind, they acquire insight and knowledge by revelation. We have the objective to justify a perfect and latent existence by observing the details of reality for evidence, with the purpose to substantiate the presumption that there exist influences upon material reality from higher realms.

It is upon the realizations brought by divine revelation that you have knowledge. As you reason with supreme reality you conceive that science and existence are calculated by potential. The source of potential is the dramatic conception of the creative universe.

The universe was designed with the intention to masterfully evolve. Our instance of reality is relative to the potential expressed and observed in present circumstance. The veil disguises the true and authentic perceptions regarding the *actual* present reality and circumstance from the enlightened perspective of a fully evolved universe looking down on us. The illusion that creates barriers to these perceptions I speak of exists because of limited, pragmatic, and discursive attitudes which are inspired in the people by persuasive public intellectualists with limited perspective and experience, as well as our own doubts that we keep because they are shared by others. Anyone can be persuasive.

Unlikelihood... is it ever considered that unlikely events occur in a specific manner because of the other perspective it is to happen as the result of a greater probability? How likely are some happenings compared to others and what makes them likely? A streamlining of scenarios which fall into various intersections of circumstance in the development of situation. The unfolding of increasingly complex incidents to remain unchecked, but only examined in likelihood only when appropriate?

Mark was always pensive. When he spoke, it is as if he were saying commands, his tone reinforced by his determination when speaking. He was shaped by the astral realms of inner creation, from the lawlessness of the supernatural environment and the netherworld.

I constantly questioned my existence and stared back at myself in the reflection. Wondering the thought, *"who am I?"* in a constant, self-defeating interrogation between my inner soul and human-defined Ego. I was the non-existence that chose to exist by the hold of an egoic vessel. I shared a dialect in a language with people, and exhibit unique but familiar expressions in my appearance, personality, and ambitions. These are the things people can relate to and understand. But I know in some way I am *alien*, and so is everyone else...

Form the former relationship between yourself and the outside existence in its abstract and all-encompassing nature. Develop and involve the psychic connection to the universe, depend on it when in search of guidance or help. Your relationship with the perpetuity of the universe makes you a variable to the control. You can change on command when you have ascended the limited awareness of the human ego.

When I became nobody in 2012, a *no-name*, I became like a feral spirit, untamed and primal. My desire for realms beyond this one is what led me to discover Mark. Later, I understood that I had acquired insight for otherworldly dimensions of reality. I was another part of my own character in these other forms of reality, and that was not Dillon. Like yourself, my ego is fitted for this world reality. My ego is constructed from world perceptions baseless to higher reality, managing to coexist with a society of its own narratives and themes.

As myself, I was no longer identifying with how I was prior, I had seen another light to myself. I learned a lot through my first year of episodes, information that seemed better fit for another reality. This reality, but after the veil is lifted if so. The veil blocks our common perception from observing hidden forces, actors, and energies.

The veil is the separator between our imagination of unparallel dimension and this present circumstance of materialized reality. The unmaterialized world is the imagination.

We all have imaginary friends and characters that linger in the opposite of conscious awareness. It is a matter of developing your imagination, then realizing and meeting these intelligent dimensions of the inner kingdom. The mind can advance its own nature with the pressure of conscious afforded willpower. It is a matter of self-control.

The significant moments in our life guide our reflection and we seek the reasoning of supreme reality. In our relationship with the existential, we can further personal development. We are free to redefine ourselves. A personal awareness which is guided to revere the greater reach of the universe as a spirit of its own right can develop a more intimate and profound relationship. The universe is of its own grand speculation. Any world you can imagine is in part of foreign existence somewhere, at some point in time.

The spiritual universe is what inspired mythologies and stories known in religion. Animism is a theme in this book, it is the belief that everything possesses a spirit, a life. This animistic connection to reality is what brought generations of people to experience profound mystical states of consciousness. We have lost the connection, and it is no longer discussed in our culture.

The relationship I want to create within you is a connection to the living universe, for the heart of the universe to beat for you. The universe acknowledges everything you have done, said, and the moments you faced and broken through. The generations of today do not expect to witness anything when they go to sleep tonight. The lack of anticipation tells us there is a lack of engagement. If you are not attentive, you will slip to be unconscious when the universe is speaking.

The people in modern society seek God as if he delivers us goods and gifts in the real world, which he does not. God does not serve our world, which is contrary. God offers wisdom, vision, and insight of another world. Create space in his name for transference between higher consciousness and our lesser collective consciousness. An increased awareness offers patience, strength, and foundation, in a universe serving as a home for various forms of consciousness. The transcended states of human consciousness will permit human beings to evolve past tendencies like aggression and entitlement.

Following the near events of when this world undergoes an increased frequency of chaos, there will be ruthlessness, deceit, and greater attempts to manipulate the world system and people. This will create pressure on people to separate emotionally, forcing them to develop a mindful and independent awareness and perception. Mark does not feel emotion as much as he feels purpose, the humanity in him before has quieted and in place willpower is emerging. The willpower animates his persona to serve a specific role and destiny. He is not behaving by simple emotion he operates from perspective holding a greater sense of significance.

I become more intelligent when I am having episodes. I say this now because I can compare between those moments and now as I draft this book. I think fast, my thoughts happen in less than a second, a characteristic of mania but also a developing cognitive trait. I go in between no inner monologue and my expressed thoughts. The term internal monologue comes to mind, your *voice* in your mind. That which is not you *at all* but is simply an egoic projection that can deceive you if you do not detach from it by placing it in appropriate perspective.

I have enhanced ability to perceive with my mind's eye which has played a role in preparing my next steps, by becoming informed from visions and insights. I became hyper perceptive and often thought in unusual and unstructured ways. My thoughts did not stem from the influence of this world. Instead, my mind operated in its own category, with the objective to unify with the supernatural source of existence.

If I became a part of my origin once more I would know all that I have not learned from only my life. I allowed myself to be influenced by the higher divine, being revealed understanding from a strong connection and foundation. If you are a control-freak, good luck.

You must submit to existence, the inevitable future and undeniable circumstance the creative universe is our master. If you are reaching for control, you only want to control your fears. You cannot control fear, you can only enlighten the fear. I unite with former existence by my passive emotional makeup, as well as with my associations, character, attention, and altered beliefs. I redefine moments of inspiration to relate myself with the higher divine, instead of my life with this world.

The Divine Universe is an existence of realms. Realms are perceived through states of mind. In configuration of mind exists the array of perceptions. Detour your attention toward feelings and pay attention to your mental disposition. Do you think the universe is mysterious? Then, you live in a realm of mystery. Or instead for example, you exist in your mind as a curious intuitive? Then the realm is shifted into the source of the curious intuition.

What if you see the universe as meaningful? In consequence it is meaningful. This is the property which makes the universe so grand in speculation.

Rather than seeing your life in the universe as temporary, start to begin to see it as eternal. In the domains of your mind exists the conscious decision to believe. The inner source of our belief is what can newly define our awareness and expand upon limitations on our mind. You are forever in thought, ...you are an eternal art.

In participating with an honest aspiration to surpass beyond your prior natural existence, you continue to transpire from something into part of everything. Becoming everything is part of knowing everything. Many diverse lifetimes

you will seek to live in continuation of the goal
to only know.

CHAPTER THREE

VISIONS OF TOMORROW

You will spend your whole life trying to be something and it never will end until you become nothing. Do not fool yourself, realizing things is a refreshing process.

Every night we dream it is like deep diving into water late in the night seeking to make meaning from an endless amount of information, uninformed due to lack of insight. More often your luck of encountering something significant is inadequate. Human history is accustomed to receiving visions. Whether in premonitions or holy experiences, in either wakefulness or amidst the nightly slumber, there exists an extrasensory connection to something otherworldly beyond our familiar perception of reality.

Visionary abilities are excited by entering certain states of awareness with the soul sitting within the mind in control, adding an extraordinary connection to the moment and your frame of mind.

In my personal experience my more significant moments of altered awareness have been familiar in the emotions I felt, relating to an insightful and personal part of my own existence. As if learning and first seeing the original artwork which inspired my birth. I have begun understanding my life.

A friend was telling Mark as they were sitting at a table on the porch later in the night, that he dreamt of Mark vanishing. Narrating the dream, he said he had gone looking for Mark. He could perceive multiple Marks going different directions, adding confusion to the situation Mark had gone missing. In the dream, he was driving and found Mark walking down a street. The friend had a gift for premonitions appearing in symbolic, or more direct manifestations in his dreams. Many times, had he been able to predict and warn of future events for his friends and family.

Did Mark go missing? Yes, a few months later. I had another intense period of my life in 2019. Several episodes of my schizoaffective disorder within a few months, at one point getting into my car and disappearing. Later, I was found in the day walking down a road, in another city. My perceptions of reality were altered with phantom physiological sensations that deepened my perceptions. I was sensitive to energies, emotions, and my own thoughts. The fantasy and characters in my mind were more alive than ever.

The instances where I experienced glimpses of another alternate reality have been numerous. My experiences when sleeping, like my astral projections, were much more pronounced and experienced at a greater level. The deepening into different realms of the imagination, going further into the abyss and challenging my fears.

I was in a constant struggle between relentless delusions, depression, and my own personal fascinations with the vivid fantasies born from my mind. I went on like this for about four months until I stabilized on medication. Mark is who I am as being shaped by these significant interactions with the living creative universe and imagination. From the strain of my rampant mind, and the distress of psychosis, I endured. Fortunately, I got the help that I had needed at the time. This period of my life added to a total of 24 months I have spent in these psychological states.

Human history, for as long as can be understood, has had the tenacity to experience the supernatural in both dreaming and in altered states of awareness. I would like to emphasize the visions experienced upon sleeping and how these visions have persisted throughout all human generations. In the Bible, several visions are discussed as occurring in the middle of night, in a dream so to say.

These are unlikely the normal dreams that our monkey brains experience while the body and mind rests. These visions and interactions with angels happening in a unique state of consciousness that extends from the bedside. They occur when the mind is not resting but when you are fully aware and separated from your sleeping body.

This other world that communicates with ours by visions and phenomena is legitimate and has informed the spiritual human collective consciousness for centuries. These experiences offer a unique relationship between us and existence. It is said in some eschatological beliefs that the people would have visions come upon them in droves during the prospective end-times.

Messages from unseen forces are signaled from within. In our private disposition, we handle the business of our spiritual affairs, interactions, and relationships. It is also this manner that we develop a relationship with the God, the divine universe. We embody this relationship both in our heart intimately and with the universe as a distinct connection to ourselves by mind.

The personal psychic affairs have no place in contemporary discussion. The personal imagination is with you in mind, it is your private expression and relationship with the higher divine of the universe. An active and present inner dialogue of reflection is of foremost importance for the maintenance and development of your soul in maturation.

When Mark looks at the television, animals, people, he perceives a different dynamic presented in psychic image and interaction. Not only does the awareness of our mind notice the material projection and behavior of another entity, but the mind may perceive an extension of inner narrative expressed.

This extra perception identifies a different reality that persists in the vacuum of potential. Time itself is the difference that separates the numerous potential states of an entity or situation centered in the realm of possibility. All that does come to occur, is meant to occur in the fulfillment of our collective time dimension.

Mark can perceive hidden potential and character in others, he noticed it in himself. I discuss this feature as the 'higher self.' This dynamic of altered perception is present also within situations, in the environment, art and music, and even in written words. Therefore, I teach a system for perception, so that your mind's eye may gaze into inner significance that is profound and spiritually awakening.

We have a choice to perceive information in any manner we intend to. If one were to unlock their inner creative capacity, they may achieve the heightened creative awareness that I allude to. Through compounding together observations of reality toward an elevated awareness, then with inner intuitive intelligence, you can reason into detail the higher reality.

I believe those that are non-schizophrenic can achieve schizophrenic-like states of mind, typically in sensitive situations, either by feeling inspired by the surrounding energy, performing meditation, or the use of psychedelic drugs. And as well, trauma and any forced detachment away from your personal reality can also result in ego loss. Loss of self-identity brings new voices to your mind. No matter how we acquire an inspired experience, we may progress toward higher consciousness.

The stream of higher consciousness, when understood as the principal cause for an understanding and the ability to communicate it in extensive proportion, is built upon self-constructed reasoning. From the higher consciousness you call upon the knowledge in your expertise of reality, able to create purpose for every intellectual inquiry from your mind. The black space within, that which is your mind, is there for your projection and access to available connection. I see a bright glowing image in my mind, I hear the next word... feeling fifth-dimensional in my knowing of time and what else, simply one question of speculation to be addressed by a magnitude of fixated perspective.

We are without anima (the spirit) prior to physical conception. We await as the precursive imagination of intelligent reality. We are creatures of the mental that are being born into materializations of the physical. Our soul (or psyche) having been equipped with anima, is able to animate our vessel, the human body.

Upon our inception into this collective reality, we are initiated with the property of animation identified by our first movements.

We are to continue to develop the spirit of anima as we progress through life, only in preparation for the next life. Anima is consciousness, it is animation. Anima is the life source that provides the process of animation. It is ambiguous, but it is also identifiable. We can live with the abstract by offering the abstract its own terminology, and with forming new perceptions we deliver ourselves into new moments of further awakening. Anything without anima is stuck in frame of motion and time. Nothing we are familiar with fits that characteristic, nothing except space.

Space itself is the mental, it is the fabric of existence. Space occupies and stays as a constant. It can be stripped away, manipulated, but cannot be created other than by the evolving Nature born from the all-natural singularity. Which is proving to be limitless.. a rapid and aware limitless that expands each time we pressure a finite understanding of it.

We will prove little to be wrong as we are captivated by the much alive, divine universe. It is only a matter of time before collective divine intervention. The universe will reveal its hidden existence and is awaiting our impending evolutions in collective awareness. Upon our eyes finally closing in on the radical light of truth and perception, the Divine Universe will jump out to be in front of our gaze.

The phenomenon of perceiving your imagination in physical reality grants you access to a new dimension of your mind. To be able to see the world and universe speak to you, as it reveals its personality in a new private connection; it is the opportunity to become closer to the heart of your soul, the kingdom of Heaven. Heaven is the eternal imagination that is full of an ecstasy that is inexplicable but dazzling with enthralling emotion. The perception of our reality stands on the informed engagement of our senses. We experience by sensation, from the auditory, visual, and so on, all that brings intellectual stimulation to the senses. We can feel gravity, we can feel weightlessness.

We are in a space that perplexes us because it is perceivably of an infinite measure and indefinite capacity, and of no limitation. Liberation is a virtue that is achieved by the dissolution of self, and the removal of our self-centered antagonism that is found in the modern tunnel vision of seeking desires and materialism. We can only liberate the universe when we are liberated ourselves. Technology is permitting us an opportunity to explore the universe, and every kid grows up curious about the universe and life.

God is centered as a response to our aspirations. We aspire in our knowledge, ambitions, kindness, and action. In response, we are offered opportunity, latest information and insight, leading us to a direction further into the developing story of creation. Think about it, are we of an intelligent matrix, and whom is the architect that opens the door to the possibility of seeing our aspirations unfold? The Divine Universe provides.

Granted significance to your reality develops the relationship of your soul to the inner domains of existence. With the initiation of having acquired additional meaning you can become one in the part of Nature. In further relating to the meaning and purpose of Nature, and by placing yourself within the natural guidance of the Divine, you can become property of God. Motivated by a heartfelt spiritual inspiration that connects you to your personal intentions toward the direction of the divine.

With the creative imagination and heightened perception, you can witness your reality with new means becoming fonder to existence. You inherit profound and new personal insight by the developing relationship between yourself and your inspired imagination. You may only understand the potential of your awareness in the moment you have first elevated your perception. To elevate your reality, engage your mental capacity to compare between lesser and higher reality. To see the difference of the two, you must further your personal understanding of the divine inspirations hidden in your mind.

You see clearly, and you have your desperate wish for connection within your hands. In the scenario that you are not presently at the pinpoint of this concept by lack of experience in heightened awareness, do not worry. You are not the only one, we all have things to say, so do not fade away.

"Who looks outside, dreams; who looks inside, awakes."
Carl Jung

Throughout life, the one thing to be consistent as a concern of yours is the way you are shaped in how you mature as you get older. We can regress views, develop new perspectives, and even change the way we think. The person we become is often a shadow of who we are today. To what light does that shadow exist? Nobody is responsible for improving their character and keeping a positive demeanor.

You must push yourself to keep mastering your character, working with your strengths, and better understanding your weaknesses. Hearing about yourself from another person is a wonderful way to learn what your issues are. I realized my temper being an issue of mine because a best friend mentioned it. The temperament of your ego is secondary to the disposition of your soul. The reaction that comes from the inner part of you is more important than ego. Be sure that inner part receives love and attention or else it may be negatively impacted.

The mind is a gateway. It is the centerfold of transference between two lines of information, that of the physical and psychic engagements. I am informed by the other side, a creeping channel of the otherworldly communicating from inward which I have permitted into my mental realm of acknowledgment. To say I have an expansive imagination is an understatement.

The imagination is not defective, many just have not achieved a control of it. I have witnessed what exists within me and had the opportunity to discover it further. It continues to persist entirely in the acts of a progressive unrevealing in which I come to learn and experience inwardly. The seat of the soul in my mind, my mind's eye is witness to the other side. It is a confident understanding that does not confound me, I am knowing and only encouraged to share.

The shadow of the anterior mind showed glimpses into the future. Mark was commanded to sit in the solace of my mind to capture every moment and detail across the year of 2012 riddled with foreign events. At that time, I directed my higher self to begin writing to prepare my mind for the day I express it. And here we have it, I have answered that calling. I have projected moments within to be later captured by the event that I myself intervened in that previous moment once more later.

I formed together the preplanning in my future development, performing a prolonged arcane ritual in the ways I thought and behaved with the anticipation that my intentions would later be expressed back to me. I executed the strategy to later receive it. In action we create consequence, even if it were symbolic and inconsequential. The universe would respond. I began the procession of thoughts, and down the red carpet they have led me to divinity. I have recalled the science of reality. I work to master in my alternative self you know as Mark.

It begins with a proposition; can I go just insane enough to preview the genius of the universe? ... Are you prepared to lose your mind? I say without mind is spirit. If you lost grip of reality, would your emotions pour out? Your self melting into the ground, the warmth of the sun felt inside your skin much like having hot and cold flashes. Except it is just warm and cozy, you were finally understood for once. The insanity does spark genius. If the mind has already traveled down four hundred questions in the matter of three days, would it know any better.

At the crisis of learning the deception of this world, the conclusions you have gathered prior become renounced and that now empty space screeches terror toward the inner soul. You shrink in despair because you realize the fear. You fear having no clue for what will happen when you fall out of your body. The idea of being vulnerable to everything makes you stammer. The submissive characters struggle with having control or being independent. The dominant characters struggle with feeling vulnerable and dependent...

The coffee spilled on the carpet already muddled with previous stains. The dog walks over crying and confused. A heart attack took your life, and it was set in time that everyone in your family had obligations outside of home except you. You died as if nobody was supposed to be around. This world is not all, there are more.

There will come a point in time as we cross into the next existence where we have choice between this world and another higher realm. Smoking cigarettes, drinking alcohol, watching television, these things make you human. Separating the world away from you allows space for your elevation to higher conscious thinking. Renouncing the habitual and our mortal life is performed by coming to terms with it, then letting go. Both must be done to come to a mutual respect toward our life and for meeting the separation by leaving it all behind. We must become trusting to the understanding that our spirits will know each other in the higher existence because the journey there is individual, it is done alone but everyone must do the same.

We live in a physical realm of thought that is perpetuated by the communal intersection of science and reason. The tangibility of science is self-explanatory by default. Further reasoning in practice guides us into understanding the functional universe. Everything is an idea, for now. If it is a measured instance of probability we can understand it. We cannot fathom the impossible, so our notion of potential is distorted by our existential immaturity. Only the mystics have witnessed God, people who have not dropped onto their knees to worship.

Is worship a form of appreciation, or is it opposite as being negligent? Worship suggests the image of God is beyond our own, that God is not of similar nature to us and able to correspond with the personal. This is a form of separation. God does not sit upon a shelf you cannot reach with your hands and arms. He is of the spirit within you, all Spirit is connected.

How can you feel the Divine when you fear – do you fear it? Are you attracting yourself toward the apostasy of spiritual connection? The disconnect where you chose to accept the condition of a God you do not understand as result of your unintelligible fear. We are not gifted when God acknowledges us, nor are we blessed. We are in one part the same as all existence and there is nothing special with us, just something that is completely natural. God is the supreme deity that is the order of the kingdom of Nature, the projection of the higher realms is Nature in transcended state. Heaven is elevated beyond the planes we coincide and beyond our level of awareness.

Upon a lucid journey, Mark was experiencing the global crossover. He saw everyone either going to lunch like it was a regular day, and those who chose to not participate in everyday life. Those making conscious effort to become separate to their past lives were able to ascend into higher dimension, eventually into light. This was performed by renunciation of the world and its lifestyle. You either stayed or chose not to. This world feeds into many desires, a prolonged period of shameless pickings into desire creates erratic and uncontrolled behavior.

Nothing that is void of goodness can sit well in the arms of the spirit. It is clashing energies that lead to degradation of Spirit into something more inferior. We come down to desires that we hold, we are the prisoners. We must find the open space to create something sacred inside which can empower us. We do this by reflecting and seeking the good that we may see in ourselves, then empathizing with that part within our self. We all begin innocently; we have neutral souls which align to a karma and a universal reputation.

Let me be direct about my beliefs. We go to realms like the ones I experience during my schizophrenic episodes. The mind precedes and follows the physical. Intelligence forms and devolves into further intelligence. The physical is a state of material conception in the mind, the reality is just an idea. Without material is formless material, yet subsisting in a realm of information as information.

We do not need the material to take place when there is the mental degree of dimension that is integrated in our reality of physical and non-physical. Two states, the physicality of the alive and the conception of the spiritual undead. Also, there is lack of state, the null.

Every soul has 'schizophrenic' capacity after leaving the body. Your hallucinations form the interior perception of your mental awareness, and you are immersed in the experience of the mental reality coming alive, of your mind becoming alive. I know it is not all fact, but it is not all wrong. It is simply a display of all communicable thought.

Your vision is focused on a presentation of intelligence, the atoms dancing in front of your eyes like static on the TV. Mark is the architect of his mind and the witness of his own knowledge. Mark created his inspired reality by understanding the divine God as source of inspiration, the divine universe that is. It offers all dimension to every thought in your desires. It knows you better than you. As the creative source of all intelligence, we need this connection to give rise to our imaginations to experience.

Following death, we become victim to our mind. The other realities are reached through gateway of time, or lack of time. Your mind would not be operating to conclude there may be something when there is nothing. And though there may have been nothing, you create something. You conceive of a divine supreme deity that was not there previously in your awareness.

The corporeal nature of consciousness and perceived reality is due to the experience of sensation. It can be manipulated by mind, then consequentially you can experience an altered reality and new state of being. We travel the mind by way of perception. Through developing your mind and becoming familiar with your internal energy, you may create a second nature of reality to interact with.

The execution in mentalism is really an unfinished art project. It cannot be mastered by another artist because they never had the original vision. What is the vision? It's the process of replicating Heaven into a comprehensive understanding, a player-defined heaven, an experience dominated by our creative imagination, but in alignment with the laws of your mind. Your ability to counteract and advance past these laws are held to your personal agency and intellectual capacity. Mentalism is a performance art of the mind and imagination.

We are a consequence of consciousness; the universe is causation. In the consequence, we are aware as beings, to manifest action and creative capacity to define our world and the universe. And our waking state has available an expanded potential. The reaction to events creates one more possibility. Determine your actions with strategy, tamed by your personal willpower and self-control. We walked down to Earth from the stars to live in repercussion of the forces of good and evil.

The present moment introduces a situational formality which is later to be disrupted by a change in events, the unforeseen. The unforeseen is the unknown of non-existence which transpires in temporal dimension from the future. Existence is noted by presence. We are born into the physical and conceived from the source of Absolute reality, that source is the transpiration of a future which leads to a perfected collective existence, the indwelling of the Omega. The evolution of the present moment guides toward new installments of the unforeseen. There are many changes to come in the way of perfection. Minds advance over time.

We are not simply present with God; we are watched by God from non-existence. The lack of engagement of the Divine notes lack of presence, but the Divine is observation itself. Look at someone in the mirror from an angle, if you can see them, they can see you. The universe does not hide, so we are always seen. The act of observation from reality, not we, determines the quantum. It does this with greater intelligence and determination than what we have in ourselves. To overthrow the discourse, you would have to present something genuine that meets divine standard.

This is a realm of potential, which is an arena of mental dimension that exists in the plane of divine intellect. Thoughts would have to transpire from this plane to be considered divinely inspired. Man cannot substitute his own inspiration to be divine inspiration, which is what must be distinguished. The individual must be influenced into action, not acting with intention to influence.

Divinity interacts from all directions offering a subliminal nature foretelling of the Divine's planned actualization of the universe in mastery. Though not presently, we are known by Spirit and that of an ethereal connection escapable to time.

Two directions of past and future exist without temporal barriers. The present moment to develop an entanglement in eternal connection between past and future, the occurrence in the spirit of God is simultaneous in event to our presence of self in spirit. When we are alive in Spirit, we reach the spirit in the Divine. It is understood by communicating within that we may develop the personal tangibility for God ...something about the word original, knowing it is familiar. Resolve your separation from original nature. You were endowed by spirit to have this capacity, but you were taught to ignore it and catch falling apples from a tree of knowledge you never planted yourself.

At the beginning stages of creation there is a greater span of evolutionary potential. Only a Nature that recognizes itself can determine its planning to represent itself in further evolution. We see wildlife as a clever evolution. The universe is also an evolution, the greatest project in existence.

We will meet our maker when the stage becomes prepared by the forces of Nature, when reality becomes alive as much as it does in the afterlife. The conjunction of possibility are two halves of potential in a binary system coming to a calculated resolution. The creator universe operating with schematics to reach a specific destination in consequence, in its preferred direction. An event with either negative or positive consequence, defined in principle perceptively to negate counterfactors, reciprocate quality, and deviate to new levels of progression in the evolving environment.

The light of gnosis is vibrating energy to create a spectrum of wavelength and color. The light itself planted a seed in the development of the foundation for a home. Of the light came the universe, because colors are of the same nature. Light is source of the transpired universe because it is visible conception, it is central awareness. The light within, that of gnosis, is the providence beginning the higher echelons of Heaven.

Remember, you are here to change the lives of everyone. Never settle for less while the planet continues to burn. We are not settled here to satisfy evil, instead we are to enlighten life with the good we encounter. We are to remind ourselves of the former realm of light and purpose, the good of which we have taken for granted and forgotten.

CHAPTER FOUR

THE GARDEN OF EDEN

God does not exist. He does not, if existing is material and physical presence is necessary to be considered real. If those qualities are unnecessary for existence in your views and all that is needed is an awareness to cultivate a connection, then you have your answer. God does exist, accessible to the boundless reach of our mind.

God is part of there and not there. Like us, he chooses to exist or not exist. His presence is called to whatever dimension of grand reality that is both engaged by an immediate desire and need for divine intervention. He is the force of intention in the divine universe, in that he is the Divine Universe creating change by intervention. The divine universe is the greater being of a supreme deity.

Time is not linear; the universe instead is a conglomerate of eternal circular time dimensions floating in the vast space environment absent of time itself. Each circular time dimension, a galaxy, is separate from others by the end of space. This is unobservable but the ends of space/time are known to us as dark matter, which is in the common intermediate that is foundation to all galaxies. Dark matter makes up twenty-seven percent of the universe and is present in every galaxy system.

Imagine a linen cloth shredded at the edges, from several strings interwoven to a few spare strings where the fabric breaks off. At the end of time, time is fragmented into non-existence, or it begins elsewhere. If attempting to leave this universal reality that is inescapable, you must disconnect from this existence and exit into the void and lack of space. You need to go into Nirvana, which is beyond space/time.

Gravity brings frames to the second, time is brought from the pulling of the time dimension by the supermassive black hole at the center of our galaxy, which is pushing matter into the direction of the future – the black hole itself. Time exits the supermassive black hole of the galaxy. Time pours into the black hole as if it is water entering a *supermassive whirlpool*. The laws of physics break down in the supermassive black hole.

Where does the time lead to? It is diffused and accelerated into the far future to eventually return to us. If we were carried along, we would exit past time, and become displaced from the physical into the immaterial reality. Nirvana operates as a blank slate with no held definition. It is non-existence, it is the imagination. The supermassive black hole is the apex of future time, it is past our present reality and leads into the non-physical imagination, which is a derivative of non-existence, Nirvana.

When entering a black hole, the laws of physics degrade into a blank, undefined state. Entering is like walking inside a hallway making no distance when walking because it is not captured as a difference in the universal physical matrix. Your distance is not recorded because of this not existing time. It becomes mental and time stops, converting to the system of Nirvana, non-existence. At this point, you enter the thought-responsive reality of the imagination where the mental and the mind constitutes physics, and your capacity in mentalism governs reality.

There is the belief in the Bardo, the intermediate state of existence that continues reality between the gap of existence and nonexistence. The belief originated following Siddhartha Gautama's death, from interpretation of the Upanishads from the Indian religious scripture the Vedas. Earlier schools of Buddhism later came to accept the existence of an intermediate state between life and death. They hold the belief that after dying, the individual would pass into the intermediate state, the Bardo. Many people have belief in an intermediate state, and their beliefs are quite like how the Bardo is understood.

We become victim to the climax of life which comes to elevate our perception of reality as we rip away from the physical world and become non-physical. This climax begins when the mind clears out of thoughts, then wanders and dissociates. Feelings then arise dependent on the individual's emotional state and gradually intensify. A good ending will end with the individual no longer caring as if apathetic towards life.

The apathy appears when we have finally become sensible to something greater that exists past death. It just makes sense at this point, which is why many pass away contently. Not many had the words to speak it in our existence here, but their dying state was cured by a greater anticipation for rest and comfort in death. This is a scenario for when death is expected. When it is sudden, then death remains a climax but unexpected. The climax is experienced in many forms other than emotional.

The climax experienced at death is also energetic. The feeling of *energetic vibrations* is understood by those who have faced out of body phenomena and near-death experiences. Scientifically understood, vibration refers to when atoms and particles are having vibrating movements and are oscillating, which is phenomenon caused by energy. Vibration is more than a term that relates directly to energy, it is also experienced by sensation. The sensations can be experienced in a psychophysical condition. They are phantom to the physical but obvious to your perception.

Through my experiences of feeling vibrations by my detachment away from reality into the out of body state, I can describe the sensation. It is like when shocked by electricity, you feel both energy and pain. Yet for vibration, you feel energy and gravity. If I placed my pointer finger on the skin of your arm and pressed it down and moved it side to side tugging at your skin, gravity is felt like your skin moving by a force but not feeling my finger on your skin. This is similar to the sensation, but able to affect the whole being rather than a part, and able to be experienced in the forms of shifting and swirling.

The Nature of the intermediate state is responsive to your thoughts, feelings, and emotions. The journey involves letting go and reconciling with the past. Your trial is against manifestations of your fear, perversion, hatred, and sadness. It is a deep and inner-invoking experience that leads you to feel every emotion involved in the process of letting go. Taken away from being your own animation of character in a physical reality, you become dissociated past the ego into other states of being beyond simple ego.

Withdrawing from your own subjective perspective, you can see through a new awareness to reevaluate your life for one last time. Upon contentment and the sense of complete resolution, you will leave behind life and carry on to an ascended form of reality to meet with others in the world of spirit. In the transcendental existence, there exists alignment to natural law.

. . .

With the Garden of Eden, God allowed a home and paradise for Adam and Eve. This home was made in the presence of God. We made a life here, to lay a foundation for our future. Our life serving us, and us serving the universe. This works in mutualism, because both the life we experience and the universe offer security and prosperity. Though, in current circumstance, that may be hard to believe.

The proliferation of deception and hysteria is igniting all ends to immediate destruction, rather than snuffing them. The universe is a home for consciousness, thus we need to protect and value our existence. As stated, our homeland exists in presence of God. If that were to be fully embraced, your cognitive thinking would demonstrate an awareness to the underlying context in which God is involved nearby. Presently, we all behave as if we are not being watched by the very universe that we watch ourselves.

Observing our interaction, the universe determines the fitness of everyone by analyzing our mental, physical, and spiritual levels of being. There are times when the universe saves us from consequence. In the direction of predestination are the events of redeeming quality and intervention by Nature, which develop over time. The regressive rationality in modern society dominates our perception and weakens our inherent ability for imagination and connection.

Holding yourself a distance away from Spirit is operating with lack of recognition for the supernatural, never permitting the observation of such forces. In our socialization into the world system, the inner creative capacity of our human nature is robbed of any aspiration to embrace the unknown. To understand the unknown, we must increase the awareness of our condition. We must deepen perception on everything. A common fear in people is the fear of the supernatural, the idea of being vulnerable to your imagination. We are terrified of what exists in our mind. We are to befriend the darkness that comforts us and honor the light that separates us from the unknown.

Creating an excuse to disguise true intention is an attack on reasoning and is simply understood as lesser deception by further distorting the perception of reality. What also misrepresents reality is subscribing to other beliefs which hold no substance and are unreasonable. When you express a form of deception, you are diverting another's ability to reason.

Lesser deception corrupts the natural process toward enlightenment. On this matter, invoking the truth may guide us toward the higher realities. We can only make the right choice when within the territory of truth. By defending the source of natural flow in self-realization and atonement, we permit the collective manifestation of resolution and harmony.

This improving quality of peace and freedom is caused by a lack of disturbance. We will one day be able to play the game of not talking and not thinking, but behaving in a new form of symmetry of human behavior. The new height of collective mindfulness is continued by a willful participation between all people. What will unite us? The will to live a good and humble life. In desperate times it will be less difficult to communicate the truth. The hold of the oppressor will weaken at the spirit of collective social reform.

When you believe, that is when you undoubtedly know, something within you finds the willpower to motivate change within yourself and awareness. You change to a higher state of meaning and purpose, feeling enlightened to an extent. The divine universe demonstrates possibility, it does not show limitation. If you want to go home, venture within to inhabit a home set in the temperament of the heart. You find home by placing your mind in a particular state of perception for understanding a new elevation in the concept of home which stems from divine inspiration. Realizing that the universe is our home and that we can never be lost will resolve a great length of fear.

To enjoy new vision of divine perception, both the mind and heart must postulate for knowledge to create an inner direction toward a new state of higher being. At some point in the overall progress of making increasing sense in your perception on reality, the experience of spiritual communion with Divine Nature becomes accessible. Elect yourself to divine inner programming and opt out of the demiurgic matrix. Make the choice to enlighten your suffering with grander perspectives than what the world has to offer. The world offers nothing substantial; it continues to exist in the realm of chaos.

Take on new meaning in spoken sentences. Find out how others truly feel, then shift the spoken into the unspoken. What else is hidden, or aware in the human psyche? A mindful awareness seeks purpose in this manifestation of a so-called "universe" ...

"The so-called universe" ... A necessity for us, the universe offers provisions to satisfy both hunger and thirst, providing a habitat for abundance and security. Home is existing in a heightened perception like the childlike imagination, and our kingdom is the glory of inspired creation, the land that holds significance. The people are lacking identity, and so, cultures develop to find identity in the land.

In regions of the world, people have found their own distinctiveness and relationship with existence. We are spiritual beings orphaned into a world with no trace of becoming, and so we identify with the environment rather than the self. Like a dog living with many cats, the dog would assign itself the inner characteristics of a cat. We find our role by knowing how to survive on the land. Ascended from the state of survival is the state of knowing. In initial stages of knowing, like surviving, we begin without a system to coordinate achievement.

Previously to knowing anything in life is living without knowledge. The next state of existence is then received by acquiring knowledge. The social complex of inner self advances to an elevated state of existence by finding a parallel in perception toward a higher projection of reality, then redefining existence with enhanced awareness. When you perceive more, you experience more. This is the law of perception.

We seek to experience more to have more to learn and reflect upon. We are desperate to be acknowledged by higher reality. Since we are lacking recognition for the basic need to bond with reality, we humiliate the living condition. Every time you are responded to with emotion, you are left with satisfaction. You are addicted to feeling understood.

Mark repeats "feeling understood..."

You look to God every day in life. In your life, unconsciously your attention scans reality daily in search for a revival of Spirit, seeking for significance with growing anticipation. We pursue that meaning because a revival of Spirit would mean there is hope. That held anticipation is a need that is never satisfied. We witness people aging then dying but never changing into more.

We can make steps to become knowing, moral, and aware. As mortal beings, we have acknowledged the reality of death. People who search for significance in their reality assist themselves by inching toward the realization of their circumstance in life being unbounded by mortality.

This realization separates the immortal spirit from the mortal body in the knowledge that we persist in a constant existence. The misfortune is not ever learning this in our life, the tragedy is never being able to learn. Regardless of other people never wanting to know, we still need the option so to never burn away. Unknowingly, we are desperate for higher meaning and purpose. Not only are people dying, so is the relationship we formerly had with our collective existence.

Ancient religion from historical civilizations were often polytheistic, having a pantheon of gods. Animism connects Spirit to nature, from the lifeless, such as a mountain, to the lifeforms of higher intelligent expressions. Historical civilizations having progressed from this unevolved human belief system began to assign deities to geographical features in the world. These gods also may be known as land deities and are the energetic spirits that are perceived to reside in dominion over specific cultural regions on the planet.

Yahweh from Canaanite religion is a deification presiding in the land of Canaan, a deity who protected the land. We now understand the incredibly revered status of Yahweh, as the most prominent deity worshipped in relation to Abrahamic religion. These land deities were worshipped by us in effort to shape the future of early civilization.

Though Yahweh was the national god of ancient Israel in part of the Canaanite pantheon, the deity persisted into monotheistic religion we know in our modern society with Abrahamic religion. To consider that our primitive perception would assign deities to significant regions of the world in history allows us to understand the relationship between humankind and land deities.

Humanity in the past could not find appropriate labeling for the observed deity, some acknowledge no name would simply identify that of which cannot be known as this greater Spirit. Though there exist many names and titles for the supreme deity, God has been previously identified as being without a name because God cannot be named. God is indescribable, no term or name can develop the proper distinction in personifying God as a unique being.

In Canaanite religion, Yahweh was a storm-and-warrior deity that protected the kingdom of Israel. A feature of land deities is they hold property over regions they are described to protect and defend. Knowing this early history of religion and the simple worldview of animism guides us toward understanding further. God was perceived in the land of Canaan and Judah by the Israelites and people made familiar with the land.

These generations developed a relationship with the spiritual face of the region. The deified land of this part of the world made appearances to the habitants, revealing new intention and purpose. The Israelites receiving this spiritual unity with the land allowed Yahweh to survive and persist through generations of written history.

Let me point out one thing about Abrahamic religion. Father God in the Canaanite pantheon is El, not Yahweh. Abrahamic religion exists in a dissonance in our modern society because to be frank, in ancient history Father God was never worshipped. There were not any temples constructed to worship El, the Heavenly Father, in ancient Canaanite religion. And, may I add, the inherent paganism of the religion headed by a supreme deity is termed henotheism, one supreme god ruling among many lesser deities.

The Israeli captives of the late Babylonian empire brought a testimony back that Yahweh was the one and only true god. The cult of Yah-weh is responsible for the appearance of the tetragrammaton 'YHWH' in the Hebrew Bible. I will leave you to debate all of this for another time.

The dogma originated by religious and spiritual experiences that fell upon previous human generations. Angels being witnessed in the out-of-body experiences, or religious visions holding symbolism, are constructions of our relationship and perception toward the kingdom of Nature and the Divine. This is the energy felt between us, and the liveliness of the environment being noticed as a real, living connection.

The technique in a spiritual relationship with the universe should be focused on an intimacy between the self and universe. Be honest and personal to yourself, as your chattering of the mind is expressed in the awareness of the Divine Mind. This communication develops your relationship with higher reality. Humanity throughout history sought guidance from Nature and the stars. In modern society, people are latched onto the leadership of politicians, hoping that they offer direction. There are people who listen for direction from the words of their peers, and there are those who focus on stillness and passive energy of the universe.

A relationship established with the material system in this world creates the illusion there are no outside forces. This develops the helplessness in the human condition, furthering our codependency with the familiar. The universe has greater control over the fate of its creation. The manner of which divine interventions take place are varied in the probabilities of unforeseen events. It is not a system of luck or of privilege, it is the predestination of those who must do things in the future, and those whose time has come. The universe shapes scenario as a deified controller, it unfolds the setting for a particular set of events to deliver. A relationship with the immaterial reality removes illusion that we are separate from our existence and that of spirit.

It is deceiving to think that we are born without an intimate and personal relationship with our existence. We are born with a sense of belonging that cannot be taken away. We are to become acquainted with deep, familiar, and mystical energies as we expand our awareness and evolve. These internal energies are fond to our souls. We are created by this universe, so we are characteristic to the workings of this universe. To be informed by the universe and its inner nature is simply to be reminded of the supreme energy from which you were born.

We are created with matter that is older than I can describe. We are intelligence expressed in advanced forms of consciousness. Let us not be overwhelmed by mundane fascinations. We must push ourselves further consciously and concentrate on becoming closer to the stillness that is in the presentation of the grand, ancient universe. We can sense when somebody is standing behind us, so what other forms of presence may we perceive?

The practice of animism as a perception shows the universe in both mystical and deified form. The vision of a relationship between all created things in animism reveals inspiration for the spiritual human collective consciousness to unify. Becoming enlightened to understand the commonality between all created is Spirit.

The manner of spirituality I discuss is a revival of the deeper inner nature that comes naturally to us as humans. This presents as a deep familiar connection that generates insight every so often. The heightened awareness in the common person is absent or minimal. Evolving the personal identity by the creative imagination is a former practice, and commonly now, identity is centered on our participation with the world system in place.

Though in prehistory, with an awareness and perception for the spirit, the human species formed an alive and present relationship with the environment. The ancient mythologies and deities existed before as the shared imagination of people, developed by their subjective spiritual and visionary experiences. The relationship that we have with the expressions of the divine universe informs our creative imagination and perception of reality.

In prehistory, people were direct witnesses to the phenomenon of the divine universe in regularity. Since that connection has become obscured, we have created a veil by perpetuating ignorance which has further concealed our former relationship with reality. We are less receptive to things we do not look at frequently. Modern society has created a wall between us and our previously held ancient perceptions of reality. The next evolution in progress of development for humankind will be when that wall has been destroyed.

The universe does not have a name, we give it one. The imagination has a home in the universe, it exists to be secondary to our eyesight.

The third eye is your mind's eye. Why is that not obvious to many? We all have the capacity to see our imagination in mind.

Deities and other entities have visited us in extraordinary states of consciousness that occur in either wakefulness or upon sleep. More than one individual can witness the same character in a vision or spiritual experience, which created a legitimacy in these characters of vision. Meditation can help to focus on the intention of connection. The integration of self within the spiritual environment creates the relationship desired.

The Divine spirit is at control as a precursive element prior to creation. It is the force expressed into existence with an intended effect. It is the sugar pill. The word *divine* inherently means perfection. The good in perfection is what is symbolized by the term *holy*. We do not casually witness good in perfection, therefore, nobody is trying to excel in being both good and perfect.

We do not see often the unordinary good, however, we may see glimpses of it in good people. And that is how we know the Divine exists in people. We know it exists in animals and creation, but without the ability to communicate it, the Divine is never fully reconciled and, therefore, is taken for granted.

Enchanted with a mystical connection, we become aware of the greatness of the universe bearing down on us. The intention for thoughts and action to be presented with the highest ethic must be delivered into the forethought of every person living on this world to save the existence of humanity. The mission of the Divine will save us from destruction. Superstitions are joined by fear and respect in belief. People hold their gods in high regard, they fear angering or disturbing them. The god-fearing nations that have risen and fallen in this world had an awareness of other forces at work in this universe.

The New Age movement shows a false light, the idealist spirituality is deviant to a grounded perception of the world and reality. It shows reality in fantasy, given the tinge of impurity that is present in the world.

It makes the leaves of a dead plant appear colored, as if you can make death pretty. It does not address the substantial concerns of what is wrong with this world. It only promotes a spiritualism developed by sensationalist trends of creative speculation. I used to look at it as a creative good, inspiring people into their imagination. Now I see that people are only getting more comfortable in the identity and not seeking to pursue higher knowledge.

Understanding that discovery and journey begins within ourselves is only the first step. The first part of the journey ends at a cliff-hanger. The drop of regard for the mundane, for the awareness to be blanketed by greater potential upon the noticing the universe when it is shown justified. The impervious truth is this is all happening for an irrefutable and definable purpose, for each moment, and every thought.

It calls for supreme intelligence to be expressed as the scheme for all creation. After one understands the universe in a passion that is beyond good and evil, our life becomes timeless and sentimental. The mythology of clashing good and evil both round the story of creation.

To master the self is an objective that should come secondary, though is especially important. Primary is the compassion you offer and effort you give, this is self-preservation. Maintaining a presentable reputation is part of our personal foundation in our social universe.

Your reputation expands the extent of your expressive willpower by strengthening your influence. With influence you may colonize the Universe with your perfect imagination. The spiritual development of the created universe is inspired by you.

CHAPTER FIVE

THE NEXT ERA

An age of prosperity, could we have it? It would have to come by a force that pushes our conscious awareness to rise above and establish a new standard. Many people are situated below the optimal standard in where their consciousness locates itself. The standard for Earth is prosperity and love for the Universe.

Most people coexist on a mental plane that is suffered and vulnerable to change. You are creating a perception of the world in your mind and living it. You are not here to make choices that lead you to change your life on Earth. You are here to change Earth by including your inner divine aspirations into the public discourse.

Inspiring the world is the only way to make revolutionary improvement. Bring the light of

Spirit from the higher domains of reality down to the execution of your willpower. Alter your willpower to benefit from your inner source, rather than directing the willpower from the egoic to benefit exclusively the mundane exteriors of reality. You fuel your motives by your choice of action and rest each night to perform your willpower the next day.

If you are centered on a journey toward compassion, mercy, and truth, you can develop the intent to guide yourself to be not only a better human but a mystic seeking a more understanding, advantageous, and sacred relationship with the Universe. Through engaging the inner nature of reality and imagination, you are thriving in ways not observed by public dialogue. You begin to create your own attitude and imagination, to become significant in your personal character, identity, and purpose. The change occurs by beginning within.

The entirety of my messaging is to enable you to embrace the universe with an introspective relationship of your own making. Develop the introspective Heavens. The meaning and inner significance behind life is best discovered with your private negotiation with the deified universe, not with some teacher. You must create your own independent understanding. Do not harness lesser understandings of other more primitive forms of information to create a pseudoscience. What should be desired is the genuine inspiration of your imagination and intellect coming together.

The relationship with existence is often characterized by silence, so do not listen for words in the silence, sense for the source of the silence. The guidance of the divine is performed through your own reflections with the light of spirit and reasoning in your mind. Like a new relationship, you progress to learn and eventually know the nature of the universe by the reasoning provided by yourself.

If you better understand yourself as a mystical consciousness, you progressively become more sensible to the underlying creative context for you as the created. The reasoning for our existence emerges from within. It is not discovered outwardly, not understood by spoken words, but by a covenant inward between yourself and the universe.

So deep within, your development in relationship to the universe causes yourself isolation. Knowing reality for what it is can be very isolating to the self. You will notice that many people are not aware of the dream. No-body notices the collective dream. We come to a common arena in the physical, though we continue to be separated by our own individual existence.

Reality is not shared by anyone; we can only witness the presence of another by mental dimension. We most often do not inform ourselves of this awareness, the fact we live life in entirely separate perspectives. And my perspective is dead. I do not come alive in the affairs of this common reality we all share by the collective social matrix, instead I come alive in the imagination.

It is as if my life was not planned to better myself on Earth, instead to better myself in participation with foreign existence. And in that perspective, I am only becoming a medium between the power of mind and the fragility of the perceived reality. Which the perceived reality we are said to share has broken on me numerous times.

When my perceived reality becomes common to our shared reality and the two begin to intersect, I receive my highest level of satisfaction. My perceived reality becomes supernatural frequently simply because it is on the context of the hidden divine infrastructure in the universal reality. The universe is not sizeable, it is a layer on an infinite spectrum of creation. Our universe is born from the all-natural singularity, which births universes in multiplicity, and this universe where we dwell is a collective realm, a singular universal reality.

The all-natural singularity is as explained in my first book. It is an infinite mass of consequence displayed in supreme variation brought into color by all calculable possibilities. It is what delivered this universe into existence. The sentience and self-awareness of our universe becoming expressible and self-actualized. The evolution of the universe is rapidly occurring. It is also just beginning. We only witness one set of possibility in this stable universal reality. A set is a spectrum from one beginning event toward another event of completion. The set is the expressed path of evolution existing at conception to realized potential in the making of one universal reality. Other sets are being expressed in alternate universes.

The all-natural singularity can be understood as this... it is a part of a grander singularity that penetrates through multiple universes. It is the center of glass cracking in the mirror of our universe. It breaks us away from this universe when it is decided. And as said, before the all-natural singularity is the active source that resides known to us as the *divine mind*, which informs the intelligent universal reality.

It is the mental (intelligent) source of science, knowledge, thought, imagination, reason, and all aspects of information made available to ever be conceived in this universe we know. I want to bring my world to this one we all engage; I want to remove the veil which conceals the hidden and true forms of reality. And this is done by a system of perception, which *A State of Mind* seeks to teach you.

Life can only end if it stops, and this universe shows no signs of ever stopping. You must withdraw from being of the temporal and start identifying as the eternal. Your wisdom will age you into the eternal, and you will no longer appear as ingenuine, but instead, the spirit you are. Appear as yourself with your original, timeless identity which exists as the core of yourself the entire duration of your transition from young to old.

Perform this appearance rather than presenting yourself in the momentary perspective of each day as it passes, with your attitude synchronized to the cycling of day and night. Your progress in realizing your identity in the universe will also help determine your evolving perceptions.

Your parents gave you a name. The universe gave them your spirit. You are an identity to both the universe and your parents. You are perceived to be a famous baseball player by your parents. The universe perceives you to be an incredibly special child-creation. Many are separate from the true authenticity of their own inner nature. It is not time for foul play, it is time to connect the human identity with the esteem of higher consciousness.

Our higher identity, the higher self some call, is the retrospective self that pardons itself into reality to call you ahead toward the furthering of your personal evolution. It is the angel on your shoulders, telling you that you are valued more any time you choose to excite your purity in Spirit. Good human nature is easily identifiable. The massive effort in good collective human nature will completely change this world. Admitting we know little, care little, and feel nothing, to come to the truth of this, we go to call upon our higher source of identity, the Divine. Rather than curse, learn to bless.

As you reform your consciousness in identity with your spirit and not feelings, you understand the self that is held blameless for all which happens to occur in your life. When you empathize and understand with this self rather than victimizing it, you can develop agency in your willpower because your mind will lead your spirit to heights of self-awareness. You live in consequence and it does not define your Spirit. What does define your Spirit are the affiliations you develop.

If you play a wicked game, you will descend dimensions further into chaos where you eventually regress away from the soul only to eventually reject it because when it is spoiled it can only give you grief. And your disharmony will leave you complicated enough to be dislodged from the collective reality all people share, they will wish you to disappear from their awareness which will force you to evacuate this premises in the universe. I advise you to be fair in your judgement of others, because if you judge them poorly you will treat them poorly, this can only lead to your eventual demise in a universe that is seeking to light up.

· · ·

The countries in the world sit in a stance of guard from any potential dangers, namely the aggressive behaviors of other countries. In a paranoid awareness and cynical reasoning shaped by the world system, we are stuck suspicious by the general good we otherwise would appreciate. It becomes strategy to move forward, the sacred becomes obsolete and human matters are placed above the State of Nature provided by creation. We are attached to the fantasy and entertainment provided by our imagination, one of the only things that continues to condition innocence in human nature.

Let our *State of Nature* be the spiritual discovery of inner self. We are to find peace by being the self in the aquarium of life and endless space. Why be so damned when one knows having it all is learning to be without and finding all within. I learned from myself because it is the self that knows.

The self knows the creator as the source of the creative and *cursive* aestheticism to the intelligent reality. We can identify patterns of creation in Nature and reach new developments toward enlightenment. An inner universe, the divine mind develops our intelligent reality. Like our mind can calculate and produce results, this universe breeds new evolutionary growth and provides constant intelligent stimulation to an ever-evolving consciousness.

A religion of the world is simply an extension of culture itself. They are just several world religions, and that is all they will ever be. They are premature and cannot conclude any of the order that they are used to create. The content of my first book goes over a few religious systems. Kabbalah is discussed in my first book, and it is a great system to visualize and experience spiritually. Though, is it fully developed as a belief system? No. It is just a system of perception that mystics have developed for the ordinary people to learn from.

The world system is not mystical. It is dead of mysticism. Now mystics are a minority group, and they live among most people. Most people do not participate in existence with a guided relationship and constant connection to higher realms of existence. Few are living through perspectives which were achieved by an ascension of consciousness to higher elevations.

Is ordinary average? Yes. Is the unordinary average? The unordinary only becomes ordinary for the mystics. I live in a supernatural environment of Spirit. God is the apex, yet not the only thing I should be concerned about. Emphasis on the last sentence, we are stuck on God. I have found him, and now am suddenly realizing my extreme thirst to enjoy his reality, rather than propping myself into an anatomical position that is dedicated to worship. It is not my lack of appreciation to God; it is the wisdom that grants me to look over the land rather than gaze into only the sun.

This is an environment of the divine mind, the mind of God. I am only trying to correct our perception and language by reordering logic to find conclusions that lead to divine existence. Prior to this moment, we have not discussed the divine existence, we have only pointed toward God. How may it be possible to find God when you have not even discovered in perception the divine existence? What evidence of 'God' do you truly know and understand, *enough* to really say that you know who or what God truly is? I know everyone thinks of a man when they think of God, and I know that because I once did too.

Ask someone who holds a devout allegiance to some religious system for proof or evidence to substantiate their beliefs as valid. They will get pissed at some point, while you continue to be the untriggered non-religious one. It is baffling watching someone grab for their rocks and guns while trying to push a narrative on everyone that they cannot even explain. Therefore, religion is outdated. It reasoned with a primitive understanding of reality.

However now, we have graced ourselves with modern philosophy, which presents the necessary and critical importance of science to better understand the real word. We cannot reflect from an ancient perception when dealing with the present. You cannot escape the understanding that still dwells in your mind. It is fact that you do not know why existence is here or what comes to occur after death. During our primitive forms of general reasoning, the afterlife and God have been developed in theory to both answer the problem of not understanding *where* we go after death and *what* has created our present living world.

A complicated question like this is determined to only be answered by a series of fluid understandings and relative knowledge, which arise from the present unimaginable into the conceivable. This is because the creation of existence is unthinkable, we are without any awareness for the unknown predicaments of reality which have not been factored as possible. Meaning that there is a grand, speculative possibility that we have at present accepted as being impossible.

Therefore, it is not considered in part of the sum of creation itself. When we are in sight of witnessing the validity of this impossible, it will cause the world to shift paranoid. This one observation whether reached by a scientific discovery or crash-landed on the planet, will lend our awareness to be heightened.

Quite frankly, you are not going to avoid the supernatural element shaping reality that is now inconceivable to us because we have not reasoned its speculation. The universal reality we know is constructed from possibility. The phenomena of the unimaginable are unanswered possibilities. These are observations we never account for or have bothered to speculate previously.

The universe has the appearance of an expression of infinity, which is of all possibilities. Therefore, every possibility must be considered before presenting an entirely reasonable explanation for the two questions I had discussed prior, those are the questions of "after-death" and of how everything was created. You ought to understand, the way to enjoying my written work is to accept that everything is possible, and that each possibility must be accounted for. If something to us is impossible, we still must account for the reasoning that it is not possible. If we do not do that in reason, we could quickly shut many doors only to realize how dumb it was to close them previously.

In part of my writing, I teach of the mystic and their relationship to reality, which does draw from ancient perceptions. These ancient perceptions have not been captured comprehensively in any one literary work, nor understood to us as being part of our living imagination. Maintaining compatibility between science and rationality meanwhile holding consideration of our ancient relationship to the hidden divine reality is not difficult, as these concepts are interconnected.

The Divine is both science and rationality, it is the source of these two. A universe beginning as the Alpha, and the universe ending as the Omega. It is grandiose as being so masterful that it is irrational to us now. A state of perfection is acquired by our universe in the prospective future, this universe is evolving itself toward excellence.

Science and its discovery are grounded on an intersectional study of any presentational intelligence, which is evident to the relation-ship between the mental and physical. Creation expresses the same intelligence as we do in our minds, this quality marked by how everything develops and forms into being. Magic and the occult are quantum by their speculation, both matching together a calcu-lated physical phenomenon with a sense of metaphysics and unordinary cause.

The only thing that could save this world is a future event in which all people increase in their conscious awareness. Where all individu-als on Earth display themselves, and participate, in a system of transcendentalism that refers to an increased intelligent aware-ness. Participating together in a life of conscious symbolic interaction. Symbolic in-teraction comes alive unconsciously, it is harmony developing. Lacking the awareness for this social phenomenon, we have not come to understand our agency in shaping the har-mony between ourselves. The actions of a few can motivate new behavior in the masses.

We are the next temporal frame of what every one person was before us, we are the present revolutionaries arriving to this life in effort to redefine the future. We exist at an in-activated potential, and the potential stems from a personal perspective so grand that it opens the eyes of the soul. The secretly locked potential dwells past the alienation of self, at the point where your ego blurs and you dissociate. It is *you* at the level of energy that exists prior to the self-identity developed by mental subconscious effort. It is *you*, the energy, that is ancient.

Identify willpower, conceive potential, and motivate your energy into action by your will. It is I who says what I am, I may be grounded in ego and that which is saying or inclined to behave as if I am heightened above clouds and that which is watching. Where my personality is vacant to definition, with myself not forming to emotion, I am in the state of energy at an unexpressed potential.

Therefore, you will not know what is on my mind no matter how deeply you peer into my eyes. My reasoning comes from no one God, because one God has source for only one perspective. The perspective of a limited and quantified form for a singular deity is inexpressible to the multiplication that occurs as it is divided into thousands of narratives. In place of my nocturnal wondering of mind is connection to the present moment informed by the divine force which varies, as it is acute to all precepts of Nature.

What do you take from as your source of hidden manifestation in the physical realm? For me, my source is inspired from the absolute height of imagination in my vision of a perfected supreme reality. We are to know the level which extends beyond mundane reality, a higher realm of intellect and transcended existence. I know from all scientific discovery that the universe is incredible and advanced. The lazy perceptions of a still and simple reality are the illusions that bar us from ever experiencing a unified worldview on worldly matters.

That all is not complicated, it is simple and stupid, which we are willing to argue. We are the animated personas, as beings with energetic expression, like the one percent antimatter in an evolving universe of ninety-nine percent matter. What if we are sourced from the potential energy which exists forever?

How provocative in a rational society would it be if scientists discovered consciousness as a separate part and feature of the human body? That *every* being of life is like animals, plants, even the stars and mountains, and itself has *consciousness* ... the creative gift to grow and expand in awareness and evolve.

I speculate that the phenomenon of consciousness is an expression of physics interacting with a respondent physiochemical phenomenon occurring in human intelligence. It is not one or the other, as it is the separated effect of the two interacting. Space/time continues to shape and evolve the functional nature of life in abundance. We are here to realize that and much more. Are we on the verge of that discovery?

We do not have a system of connection; we have systems of separation. An intuitive should be able to see that. We define everything into our own semantics, slowly creating a rigidity in our common sense. We can express more than words, emotions, and thoughts. We express energy, which can transform into anything it is offered to imitate in property. We can transform into whatever we desire. The strength is the desire, it can lift more weight the greater it is. The strength for desire is created by personal aspiration. If I create that aspiration to look at greater heights of awareness in this book, will you desire it even more greatly, and will that offer your mind to become witness to anything I discuss?

For a period of several years in my life, even up to this point, I have had the desire to experience unusual psychological states. Being given my imagination to set in my own hands, only for it to later be taken away. I chase the magnificent states of mind. Psychic forms of being, displacing oneself outside the sense of common world reality.

Dissociating from the allusions created by our world system and creating my own. My inner light of this galaxy, showing the colors of another galaxy. The disorganization of self into a pool of ideas, thoughts, and feelings, to later be reframed with new personal perspective. To show a balance and fortitude in my personal dedication to the divine universe. Both light and dark, working together by an elect to retain the necessary equilibrium of all forces.

Do not look at my personal knowledge, thinking I am creating this moment to be something proving my point. I am indifferent to my belief system, and the thoughts I share. I did not find this knowledge; I am not the creator of this intelligence. I simply realized it and expressed it with these words, using the language to which we are accustomed.

Can English describe everything? The short answer is no. Although language is progressive and shaped by the moving cultures. We are adding more insight to our collective existence with the increase of knowledge and perspective. It is now that will always exist, and this moment is premature.

We are undeveloped to handle weapons of mass destruction, do not leave the armed gun around the toddler. We all know this, except those cast with an ego fitted for a superior and not the present inferior. Admit you are not correct about everything; we need to continue refining and revaluating our beliefs. I say, as advice, keep to a progressive spirituality.

The concept of private property creates condition for an evolving separatism among civilized countries at large, expressing division to the general demographics of the global population. In this country we must buy property in a game of feudalism, while funding private interests and agendas with our tax revenues.

All of which we share with ourselves and to others is the essence of the collective consciousness. The inner nature of the mind is sometimes equipped with the same demons but different angels. We find the heart by seeking love through others, for us to develop the love we give to them by our admirations, developed from our personal philosophies and expressions. Action declared by thought make our inherent virtue come alive to act out will-power to conquer enemies and gain further territory for those we love and protect. We are not fighting our world neighbors as we are at war with ourselves, with the corrupted human nature. We share property in life and the world. Though we live in a constant state of scarcity, lacking necessary perspective of the spiritual, and instead we aim to please the material world.

John Locke has his own idea of a state of nature. John Locke stated that the natural state of society is a state of nature in which there is absolute freedom and equality, bounded by the law of nature. Who could be upholding this law of nature? At our modern developments in society, this would be the police. Though what determines the law? The basic and necessary needs for survival, prosperity, and creation.

These are the needs of the people, not the needs of the state. A constitution to reflect the individual sovereignty having freedom, independence, and liberty. The state is not represented by the people who organize it, but the state is to be represented by the powers invested in the constitution.

To truly be without bias for a constitution, it would have to be divinely inspired. Though we must understand what has motivated our history to survive onto this point, the moments of inspiration which transpired among the masses when people performed collective reform to enable the condition for future development of society and civilization.

This process of reformation as told within history is essential for the collective preservation of our world. We must be willing to reform our ideas, beliefs, opinions, and morals, to be capable in achieving further toward an enlightened society. Individually, we make the change in ourselves upon making the realization of what is wrong in the present moment. What wave of evil is developing the momentum of influencing all people? In what ways can we work together to hold onto our common values and morals?

The divine source is impersonal to you but is the universal force that affects everything including you. The mirror that every soul can investigate, and all see the same image. The image of God. It is not your reflection that is the image. It is the image created in your mind's eye when you see the hidden view of our universe, the image surfacing within divine perception. You are a projection of a new existence. You are one of the forces of willpower in the creative universe. At the root of self is the essence of willpower. Therefore, we pull from deeper within our self as begin our attempt to become bolder.

The inner self cast by light and pulled away from a defeat happening within. You are a mess inside, but you are in a natural presentation that is organized. The force that straightens the mess out is your redetermined force of willpower. An execution of willpower molds your image to reflect the inner emotional efforts that occur inwardly. By will, you raise your voice.

As well with your will, you show affection toward another. The execution of self in personal representation of character is willpower. Your willpower changes the inward chemistry of self. The variable in this circumstance is desire. How greatly you desire to behave, believe, and act, is a benefit to your individual willpower. A person may dream to go to outer space, and if it is greatly desired, then they will dedicate many years in making every decision necessary to achieve the goal.

What do you desire? I assure you, whatever it is, it will shape your actions, decisions, and behavior. If it is money, you will become stuck to the constant fixation you develop for gaining more money. If it is exercise, you will seek new ways to train and test your body. Your endurance is one of the qualities determined by the personal fitness of mind. To endure for something that you desire is one thing alone. You also change for what you desire.

You can achieve a massive shift of self when you desire something that is unknown to the former self. If what you wanted was hidden and higher knowledge, your desire is then knowledge alone and nothing less will suffice. To better know, you would understand you would have to become the person that knows better, following consequence to lead you to that point. A part of yourself prearranges yourself for the inevitable sacrifice of the self that is learned in ego.

These higher planes of knowledge require complete dissolution of self. Your branding of self cannot and will not matter in higher dimension. The higher planes are elevated by the stratification of knowledge. To achieve higher planes, you must encounter insight from the otherworldly. This may be achieved by engaging in unusual psychological states with your performative willpower. The unusual offers new dimension to the present inquiry of our awareness. We are controlled by a free-will that is dynamic to our present accumulated knowledge and understanding. If we are not presented with a knowledge foreign to this world, we act in only the influence of this world.

You are speculated by the Divine Universe when you encounter knowledge. Knowledge is at the base of willpower and the universe ponders what you are going to do with the knowledge. It will allow you to do remarkable things if you prove to be capable and resilient. It is with this understanding that we move to prove an example of ourselves. In a world of symbolic interaction, where people follow trends in behavior, you yourself must be a trendsetter to be recognized. And those that become so are to be remarkable in history.

CHAPTER SIX

AWAKENED STATES

As you read, I will come from within the common to speak into your mind. Hear my voice in complete thought, bold yet translucent. Your unconscious thoughts and beliefs attempt to project shade of distinct color to my light. My light is purple, just slightly deviated from the white internal source. In consequential reality, we create the mental in our expressed conceptions of reality. We observe the consequence in singular form, and we envision reality with our biases. The mental projection of your mind is your prison. Discover the hidden exit.

The light of my mind exists in a private corner that is toward a far-reaching corner of space, in a place of parallel dimension in the universe. A dimension of new imagery. One of many varied representations to express physical space, existing to create perception from now, to beyond space/time. Out of the box, everything is displaced beyond the shared reality. There is no real structure, there is no chaos. Non-existence is unformed and stable, with dimension there exists the rigid nature of the creative universe.

The non-existence is only a parallel dimension, a timeless mirror in which we peer into. In response, the mirror projects our thoughts of what may be displayed to our mind. It remains at the capacity of your potential in the mental. As we begin to see the universe as a mental manifestation, we will begin to climax in our human nature and slowly become something abnormal, something deviated beyond the human nature we know today...

Everything in this present universal realm dissipates into organized chaos, even at times unorganized, this universe is what I term as a *chaos universe*. I have alluded in my preceding writing to a previous-something universe where everything came together in a cocreation of harmony. That previous universe is what I term as a *harmony universe*.

Physicists state this present universe has time moving forward. This is a part of the reason it is a chaos universe because it is open to indefinite possibilities and continues to evolve embracing that multiplicity. In a harmony universe time moves backwards. Therefore, everything came together in cocreation harmoniously. Visually, it does not appear as what we may think of when we see someone walking in reverse in our perception of how time evolves backwards. It is everything moving forward and traveling into patterns and synchronization. This progressively degrades potential in the quality of free-will with the evolution of a harmony universe. A harmony universe is a dispersion of awareness and existence coming together from non-existence into uniformity of existence. In this regard, a chaos universe is the opposite.

The chaos universe is uniform existence moving toward diffusion, presenting chaos. It increasingly adds potential to the quality of free-will in collective Nature. A chaos universe is an expression of the fully conceived state of the harmony universe that came before.

The supreme conception of a harmony universe is that its existence is slowly brought into an all-natural singularity. The maximization of energy in a harmony universe at its supreme form condenses into an all-natural singularity and then converts its equivalence to mass. This equation is $E = mc^2$. The developed mass then reverses time (backward to forward) and becomes what we understand as the *big bang*. A harmony universe does not have matter. It perhaps has antimatter in place of matter. Harmony universes exist as precedents to chaos universes.

Both chaos and harmony universes hold appearance of moving forward not backwards, although the two have polarizing directions in time. A harmony universe is a conception of existence, which is born into a chaos universe as manifestation of conceived existence. You may be able to notice we are presently in a chaos universe. A harmony universe comes together, and a chaos universe moves outwardly.

The two are parallel universes. As the two are linked by the all-natural singularity, there are moments of synchronicity of chaos in each. However, the primary nature of the universe is characterized by which stage it is at, conception or manifestation. In a harmony universe, chaos is internalized as something that can only be expressed by an individual. In the chaos universe it is the same, harmony is only expressed by the will of a person.

A harmony universe is conceived by surroundings which consist of undefined existence. The imagined material which takes place in its conception is delivered by the divine mind as its source of information. The divine mind is centered outside space/time and between the innumerable harmony-chaos universes. The divine mind defines through its awareness the undefined existence.

The divine mind is informed by the chaos universe which bring about new possibilities. The chaos universe expands, but where does it go? The universe continues to span across all direction until the all-natural singularity withers away when it has no more output to create from the preceding harmony universe.

Once a chaos universe dies, the divine mind takes information from its existence and then repeats the process of the parallel universes and conceives of a new harmony universe in the same existence. The cycle in reincarnation of the harmony-chaos universe repeats.

. . .

Enter the gateway to my imagination and see more. I am a scribe of the Spirit. Know my self as Mark and witness my territory. I went

from nothing to now, a man living with an alter-ego, enveloped in his own portal of
imagination, half-present with you and half-
present in another, personal dimension of reality. The self being developed with
heightened awareness and perception on reality. The identity of self being born entirely
from our inspirations of thought.

You may be curious about the ranking of
Mark. He is a director, a dream director. Mark
came here to create a direction and new out-
comes. Mark did not make the choice to be an
enlightened visionary, he was pressured to be
so because of the lack of vision in the world.

He is his own sovereign character, but we all
know the role has yet to be filled. There is desperate need for someone who is radical in their
perception but will continue to insist that their
perception has nothing to do with them personally. An actor being brought to the stage to
begin the discourse that leads to an ending that
was beyond the expectations of the audience.

Lurking in the catacombs of the unseen, is a
hidden participation within an internal dimension of reality. There are not simply
dimensions of the outside, there are the dimensions within. They exist beyond, toward
the inner dimensions of the imagination. The

ultimate perception involves more than one reality. It involves all in your imagination, the plausible existences all to be encapsulated in the potential of your imagination. We are here to create foundation, to start a path toward a heightened universal awareness.

If your dead father were watching you during a few moments in your life, would you be aware? No. You would not have been aware of such. However, what if your awareness encompassed the foreign and unique importance of all events that exist at a potential on the level of hidden detail in reality? The interaction of mind and spirit. We are obsessive with the perspective there exists only physical engagement. We are rarely ever thoughtful toward the interactions between mind and spirit that occur within our consciousness.

Awareness is precursive to sight. You may see a signpost that appears to be a stop sign commanding you to slow down to a stop while driving, but until present awareness catches up, do you really see? Our visual awareness is conditioned to be informed by eyesight for something visible to hold any significant meaning. This means we cannot understand what we lack awareness for, even if it is obvious to our personal observations.

We are conditioned by the mundane perspectives in our mind. And back to the idea that we could be watched by a deceased loved one, did I pull that idea from a movie? No. It is a speculation thought of by many. I have said before and will repeat, you will find a lot of your irrational suspicions about the nature of reality hold reasonable concern.

Nothing inherent invalidates the speculation you have for spiritual reality. Though imperceptible, much exists beyond us. By changing your perspective, identifying with a new source within for guidance, and being desperate to look with new eyes, your spirit becomes unhinged, and reality begins to shift dimension.

The inner world can be irrelevant to our society, it may thrive inside of you, but you will never find a proper moment in a conversation to discuss it. My imagination is unexpressed, and I am sharing my vision of it. One day, the imagination will become expressed when humanity has transcended to elevated levels of collective awareness.

In ancient times when humans were still feral and untamed, they lived with a dreamlike consciousness. By constantly being in the moment surviving, there was no effort in awareness to realize a future. All that did matter was exactly what I emphasized throughout this book. Maintaining an extremely acute awareness of our reality, begin to sense for the subtle events happening. Awareness guides your attention, and your attention creates a relationship between the mind and anything that is perceived.

My experiences have shown me an alternative form of spirituality, a spirituality I have learned by my own perspectives and perceptions. It is not meant to be understood as practical. It is having an awareness of a fully advanced, thriving universe, and seeking to have a personal relationship with it.

Befriend creation as it exists. We are existing in the sphere of Nature, and the world of Spirit is the sphere of the imagination born from mind. We are stratified by degrees of awareness. We are numerous identical souls, but we each all know something another does not.

Beyond the veil is a much more alive universe. There exists a phenomenon in physics which functions to disguise the true physical state of something prior to observation. When we observe something of an unfamiliar (or familiar) significance, it corresponds with us by entering our minds and awareness. It is calculated by the evolution of potential and a predetermined Nature.

We perceive it at a present state of what we think is possible. The divine mind is the intelligence present in the creative universe, expressed to determine Nature. With no destination other than itself excelling toward excellence, the divine mind may change its mind to put it in laymen's terms.

As the main form of sentience for the universe, it can be persuaded by us and engaged in different manners. The mind and reality are both linked together. There is a veil which suppresses our inherent capacity to perceive the unordinary, and to evade the suppression, we must demystify reality. There are all different dimensions and times in the *present* moment we believe in and engage...

If we were inaudible, then we would communicate into the universe by mind. Though we can speak and discuss, we still voice our thoughts in the mind as well. The process of thinking without having an internal monologue is the manner of perceiving the mind with direct changes to the state of mind. With one, the changes to your mind occur indirectly as the voice takes the precedent to invoke change.

The subtle nature of the universe in interaction occurs at an emotional level. The mute universe communicates like sound that does not reach the lips upon forming intent, happening deeper within. Our psychic interactions exist beyond the immediate surface of our awareness, beyond the short distance of our general awareness, nearer to the less noticeable processes of our intellect, even though action is all that matters. We simply have words to partner with actions, to make them matter even more.

Whether we fall to the demonic or ascend toward the celestial is dependent on the manner we engage to the force of intention. Is it with the desire to love, or the desire to disturb? I am not here to simply love; I am here to disturb the demiurgic reality that has captured the attention of so many souls.

It was in the moments you had with me when you chose to not speak that I was able to heal. Targeting the inflamed nerves of my emotional being with your sight of empathy brought healing. You cured me as an outsider, and you brought me to paradise. Your chosen perspective made mine look sufferable and lazy, why did I not have this drive before?

At large, we are actors in the drama around us of cosmic proportions. Nature tends to creative aspiration. We will, for several millennia, shape our universe in making. We are at the grand proportion by potential, though not by the incident of which we came into being and becoming. We are great anomalies appearing in energetic and intelligent expression. We are the tides of the universe, making change to further shores where we reach.

Exit the mind and then be forced to reenter the mind surrounded by a fog with its resemblance in your mind. Things are unclear, and you see your surroundings but cannot discern them from reality. The surroundings begin to shift and vibrate. They begin to pull you in all directions. The awareness that has taken upon itself as fog then begins to twist and turn, swirling, forming a wormhole.

The wormhole shifts into your perspective. You peer down. As it fills your awareness, you begin to see everywhere in one time. As you look to your left, your sight can no longer properly express what you are perceiving. It all becomes meaningless, and you feel within an incredible importance residing inexpressibly. Everything in your sight starts darkening at the edges of your awareness, and then all you see is nothing.

The mental component of your being is wiped blank. Nothing remains that is familiar, especially unfamiliar is the remarkable sense of knowing accompanying you. It remains to be almost familiar. A lit candle drops from above your gaze. At a point in the descent of the candle, you start to awaken.

Why deny you came from this, and why do you feel disheartened to be shown an eternal life? You wither away in fear while in your birth it was different. In your conception, your nervous system formed by mystical phenomenon in gestation, allowing you to feel. Then bones came together and gave rise to appendages that evolved into tough flesh. You were made to walk at your own will. Yet now you behave as if vulnerable to any simple difficulty, you are broken by little. It is clear to me that you were weakened.

You were lied to in life and forced to swallow any disappointment. As you are shaped by this world, you are inferior to supreme reality. You must be able to behave and to be energetically strong and simple. The attitude of your peers enforces you to meet expectations with your ego. You must find your capability to withstand the pressure and guilt. And they wonder why you do not cry while the days darken, but it is because you are fed up.

Enlightened states are accessible to you, in the one moment that you willfully choose to disengage the demiurgic matrix of the world system. That is the state of suffering. The matrix is not mass media, politicians, or your sworn enemies. These others are simply actors playing a role in the social matrix.

I discuss organized society as a social matrix because of everyone together perceiving a common value in the symbols we associate together, everything with assigned identity in a system of classification. The system of perceived existence created by the world is a false light. The curtains of the true existence are closed, it being mystified by our lack of consideration.

We operate by symbols. We look to objects, people, and beliefs, together in an organized system which we utilize to discern our reality. At one end, receiving opportunity to understand and gain knowledge, at the other end is the imitative reality formed by our social matrix. It offers you false hope, often leaving you in disappointment.

The imitator of the Divine is the demiurge, the creator of our false world system. The demiurgic persuasions are disturbances to harmony, by attempting to lead attention away from any reasoning toward enlightened perspectives. The barrier keeping us away from our higher intellect is caused by all lesser deception. The several times that you have confirmed into your mind a lesser deception furthers the demise for yourself as fallen consciousness.

Deceptive ways of perceiving truth and reality do not account for the need to reason and justify. What may have been shown to you as a practical belief and perspective on an issue may be rendered to not be practical or helpful in the end. Me, you, and everyone else are susceptible to harmful thinking.

People think that something is worth believing in if it is true. There are various shades of truth we may understand. We even have phrases of speech to explain this. There is the hard truth, which comes with a private confrontation. A personal truth that is honest with your own character. A loving truth that is an observation guided with love. And, a deceptive truth which is the dissuasion away from truth itself.

Above all knowledge is the need to reason. There are many truths to choose from. Hence, the divine truth will be known as being in the realm of holy perfection and natural law.

Any system constructed by observation for matters in the social and material reality can be potentially devastating. If there is a proposed way of correcting a perceived wrong in social and material reality, it may lead to division. There is an attack on Nature and the natural. There is nothing wrong or disingenuous about people in general.

The greater length of deception is how you can spend your whole life thinking in a world system and never thinking about anything else. That is not natural. It is more natural for us to have a grander connection to reality. A connection to be perceived in the physical, mental, and energetic. If truth was always so obvious, why can it be so hard to see?

Not all the truth is obfuscated away from us because we ourselves are lacking intellectual capacity. The true nature of this universe can be understood by reasoning. The presently unknown is shrouded knowledge. It is not reached by us because we shun any attempts to do so, because we reason that we cannot know *for real*. So, the illusion of doubt works as a trickery.

We can reason with our existence and know concretely the nature of its great works. We can have new experiences that guide us further into understanding. The best perspective I can detail for you would allow you to come alive in the awareness that you are present with an alive universe. It is not so dead here or out there. Find contentment in a humble awareness while knowing the potential is vast.

A State of Nature is an open realm of the plausible infinity in mind which is sought out by creative aspiration and the revival of spiritual autonomy. It is the authentic nature and state of creation that we adapt to, to reawaken enlightened society. It is a speculative social and spiritual harmony, manifested from stillness by willful participation with natural elements of our life. Everything in the universe is as it is going to be.

We are to embrace our divine motivations and are to no longer reject the natural human ideals for a posture of intellectual poise for a construction of worldview. Instead, we should strive for a divinely guided collective aspiration to create a full and enjoyable ecosystem of harmonious culture blended by the reaching towards primal good and the beauty of the heart and mind. Having individual security and good wellbeing allows for a person to discover and effectively reason the guided progression by all-natural forces expressed in balanced co-ordination. Whereas the spirit is housed in the mind, the mind is placed within nature. Know that the Spirit comes through the reasoning of Nature.

I would like to emphasize phenomena as the events of the sporadic and unbelievable be-coming visible in an objection against the rationale of modern speculation. What was thought to not exist, becomes observable to be believed concretely. As creatures of observa-tion and inquiry, I state we are inspired by further understanding the intellectual domi-nance of design present in the universe. We are seeking the divine infrastructure of Heaven in the Divine Universe.

In spring of 2018, I was in Miami on a date with a guy I was talking to at the time. We went to the club as I had bought us tickets to see a trance music performance. Listening to one of my favorite trance artists, I was ecstatic and enjoying the emotion of the atmosphere. I al-ways felt weightless in the sounds that transpired, the melodies and synths that created sounds synthesized from the creative imagination and sound production, a modern symphony of flashing lights. I met this lady nearby; she was Brazilian and had the accent. She was on a research grant to study trance music, to study its effect on the human psychology.

Unfortunately, I did not keep up with her or the outcome of her studies, though I am confident I understand how trance music affects me. It fuels my imagination, helps me create new perceptions. It puts my mind into elevated states where an increasing creative capacity is introduced, along with elation and feelings that shadow the overtones of the music.

I listen to music to achieve heightened psychospiritual dispositions because it arouses positive emotions and does great benefit to wellbeing. Music is of beneficial use when exercising, writing, or another method in which you seek to achieve exhilarating or creative states of consciousness.

I have experience in extraordinary realms which were offered by my departures from reality while in unusual psychological states. There are those of us who understand the mental realm as being a thought-responsive environment.

We change subconscious dialogue with will-power to reflect a difference in the discourse of our personal narrative. We make up our mind with emotional energy that is evolved by new levels of knowledge and wisdom. Insight formed within and direct experience are two levels with which we channel new intelligence to awaken our minds. Knowledge cannot be robbed from hearing another's perspective; it must be sought after within yourself.

We all have encountered various experiences. Some of us have had different experiences others have not had. Each of us speak from our personal experience. And often, people approach others with apprehension and their own rational. We do not exchange the experience of another for new perspective very well. We can only be influenced by our own new experiences.

I cannot prove the inconceivable truth of matters separate in a realm of thought. However, I at least can bring them to your own speculation, for you to question. This can only bring more awareness to a subject. Higher awareness grants the perspective and higher perception necessary to conceive of truth. This information sits on a plane that cannot be reasoned into the mundane world, as it is insight you can never properly express. This is called higher knowledge. And it is a degree higher to emotional knowledge/intelligence, which is understood in our emotions and communication.

These higher plane (or level) understandings do not have words for them. It is like thinking with your mind, it is clicking at your spasms of perception guiding you to the higher and more appropriate planes of awareness. The world, as we learned, does not sit in that plane, it is declined by value, left out of its basic explanation.

· · ·

Dip the lights low, let my mind peel back and my eyes phase out. Have my skin ripple as it folds away, my bones fragmented, and my essence of self be all that is left. Curious to speak knowing it is pure energy, my projection of formed intellect responding to any inquiry that I want to question and reflect change. I shape the spoken words with my passionate heart clutching its pearls and demanding you to understand.

Lively moments to an old soul reliving youth in the days of a young universe. Any moment I have impacted with grace to inform the collective of a new form, a dance, a ritual where we all no longer participate with each other, but go our separate ways to higher realms.

Awakened states allow space for the presence of personal conceptions of Spirit phenomena and affairs of the otherworldly. These altered states of awareness help clue you into understanding the premise of our human potential and the fully realized state. The fully realized state would be the point which you have achieved the necessary knowledge for you to have access to a new perception that permits your private beliefs to recognize supreme reality as it exists.

The realized manifestation of supreme reality in our world and beyond is an extension of the infinite potential that surrounds the evolving universe. It is the end picture we all did not know we wanted to see, and it is what our ignorance is struggling against for nothing.

The world has grown to compress perceptions of a holy divine into a deity. We see it expressed by living testimonies of people, people saved or intrigued by their encountered knowledge. We have unsuccessfully reduced the Divine into a character and idol. Questions remain. It is my belief that the Divine is the spiritually transformative and divine energy seeping into the universe like yolk pouring out of a broken eggshell.

None of us started with perceiving God as the divine force that emanates in creation, but this perception is traditional. The Divine is an exterior force as it is not "God" but instead the *force* that works within Nature. It takes force to form change, and that is why the Divine is a necessary control variable.

In quantum physics, nature determines the resulting state of something prior to observation, as if an algorithmic universe, but present in personality and intention. Divine intelligence acts through Assiah, the world of action and forces, to invoke change in progressive creation. It forms a Nature that creates the universe *the way we all wanted it to be created*.

Within the mind is immeasurable space and outward exists an expressed definition. How expansive is the distant and creative fantasy which is developed by our imagination and its capacity?

I contain stars, galaxies, universes, worlds, stories here and stories beyond. There is no present physical expression of what exists in the mind. However, there is a mental dimension you attend to in your mind. That is the dimension you continue evolving to deliver your existence to higher reality. Your relationship with reality.

With minimal effort, I can take an experience and immediately reflect it toward my personal worlds. This allows me to take added meaning from situations and the world, and I reflect the understanding I have of my inner world and compare it to my living experiences. I observe for signs, patterns, and evidence of the divine to feed my curiosity and hunger to know something greater and more profound.

I live inside my imagination but participate with reality. The two are both synchronous with the ways I think and interpret my living experiences. As I have become developed to be part of my imagination over time, I am waking up every day with more answers as I slowly depart from an ordinary understanding of reality. I do not need to be visited by the grim reaper to understand the second nature of reality.

. . .

The curtain is separated, and you are on the stage of the cosmic drama in an environment. The changes in scenario on the theatrical stage are performed by the actors and the *stagecrew*. The stagecrew at work is not witnessed but we see the work after the impact is left. There exists greater influence on our reality than the influence of our own making.

When perceiving the presence of otherworldly forces once the light of the stage has been dimmed, you know nothing of the hidden support behind those forces. We are not discussing a ghost in the room. We are considering the divine force creating action in butterfly effect. The controlling force is from the highest level of intelligence existing in an unknown department of the universe.

Whether your performance onstage is purely improvisational or a guided narrative depends on if you know the script at hand. In the next life you will come prepared already knowing your lines as an actor because you studied the script before. The story unfolding is going to be different than the stories of previous lives if we evolve from the metaphor I am presenting and its lesson of ourselves lacking awareness.

The stagecrew is an interesting part of the metaphor and worth expanding on. Forces in the universe interact and shape the environment. We are 'forces of being' ourselves as we are conscious at the front of the stage. The work onstage would not progress without the guidance of the forces that await in the backstage. These forces know the script, the plot, and they know their part in the universe. They are not the characters of the story, but the functional participants of the divine universe. We are not alone. There is a backstory that is set apart from this life as it is the former existence holding greater authenticity.

The forces of transformation in the universe make intervention at primary opportunities developed by consequential reality. The Light is the force of awakening and awareness which breathes knowledge into the soul. We are beings of light. We are animative, energetic beings that take part in the emptiness placed in the essence of life. We are reactionary measures of consciousness that develop *anima* or spirit in our vessel. In the mind effected by intelligence, we are to evolve and calculate new possibilities within the formerly meaninglessness, and here to propagate new dimensions of revealing potential.

Mark would witness the Divine's kingdom in a fashion of contemporary design, a ruling and hierarchy modernized. It was fit for a New Age. It is the authenticity of before yet fortified to be of a constant light that stays in the present as a kingdom possessing eternal relevance and appeal. This kingdom had a role for Mark. He has his own spin on this and what he must do for this universe. He offered his shade of dark to tint the light as a new wavelength. The lessons of now and the past sculpted his hugging embrace for others and the clenched fist which he waved at what he personally disfavored.

The way I perceived the Divine's kingdom I admire. I do not see the ways of which history has shown the design to be, in a form of archaicism being impractical and unreasonable. In fact, I see it in a novelty of Godlike intelligence. Heaven as a government of spiritual creation is the perfect system.

I do not personally know every aspect or mechanism which it features but I am as familiar with it as we are with the governments in the world. It is alive but behind the scenes, unbeknownst to our world affairs. It oversees without a touch. It does not interact because it is supreme and defines order in the universe. It is a definition for which we attributed a word. The motif (or reoccurring theme) of the kingdom we know in the world is the expression of our fallen imagination. The Divine's kingdom is precursive to the consequence of creation. The demiurgic-controlled realm in which we dwell remains in a fallen state receiving the blowback of all good and evil. We exist in disorder.

The Divine, its kingdom in Nature, and the mental universe are not dictated by the world system. Political and religious leaders operate in demagogue fashion deceive by their words. We submit for more suffering in this realm, which is a work of the demiurge – the false creator. We agree to more time of being deluded into the present dimension of suffering by being in bed with the antichrist.

Leave... Leave! You do not belong in the system of false hope and light that the corrupted suggest is good. If a leader tells you it is safe here, turn away! Nowhere is safe in this lesser dimension of reality, the realm of suffering and chaos. It is within the Divine's kingdom that the Absolute reality remains in eternal security and abundance. We are estranged from our former creation without the Protector. We learn from the reckoning of our peers and ourselves, and we know what it means to suffer. We will never leave home, but we will transcend the fallen state when we are enlightened on the knowledge as to why we are here not to only suffer, but to be.

From the waking state we descend to the astral state, from physical to mental reality. As our conscious awareness begins to cease, we experience observation at the level of subconsciousness. The mental plane leads to the unconscious. A step lower to the mental is the temporal which is the feature of time. You may stay in the mental on the foundation of temporary as if in a dream that lasts but only for a long moment. At the end of the mental and temporal plane into the void, you come to divisional non-existence.

The truth is absolute and divisional. It is not open for interpretation as it remains a sensible fact. The truth is shadowed upon by many but remains confused by their lack of direct experience and inability to communicate it with depth and detail. The truth is held in every person as it is encountered once before. The truth is found in a specific perception, a state of mind. It is found in moments of realization, releasing of stress, and by ascending the mind to new peaks of higher insight and wisdom.

The soul is momentarily consumed in the light of inspiration. We can be inspired into better perspectives, moods, words, and politics. The emotional and moral decline in global conversation makes the world erratic, agitating the state of human nature by creating space in uncertainty, developing it into despair.

CHAPTER SEVEN

SEEKING TRUTH

I genuinely long for my schizophrenic experiences of the past. I miss them when I lay down for the night. I perceived other realms and worlds that were so beautiful, diverse, unique, intricate, and best yet, they were accessible to me from my mind.

These fantasies came upon me so eloquently, all connecting and creating imagery and stories within my mind. It was self-fulfilling with the focus always centered on myself only. I could involve myself with whatever I wanted as anything was always available at any instance of time.

Purgatory is a gripping and sluggish reality, everyone in hospital attire, walking slowly in absent directions through the hallways.

Though in purgatory you are simply in rehabilitation for that purpose before you continue in the afterlife. Where you can go when you have been rehabilitated after death is way more exciting than anyone can fathom presently. Where you go is among infinite roads toward the predestination that is your highest potential in existence.

I can no longer go off medication as I have almost lost my life in many manic moments. It is not good for me, but I do value the experiences I have had in the past. I have spent many months now cumulatively in a manic and schizophrenic state, not all in a consecutive timeframe though.

I miss my schizophrenic experiences, always have. I really enjoyed the elements of fantasy and the very alive, otherworldly realms that I would perceive. They were my entertainment. I enjoyed the unbelievably beautiful worlds and stories in my perception and interactions. It is like an introverted heaven. Though also hell, as I have dealt with demons before and hellish realities. I witnessed and observed so much that it is hard to ever both fathom and express coherently.

Not every schizophrenic has the same experience, but it is a very severe and disabling disorder that takes much effort and time to ever find a happy place. There are many homeless people on the streets with untreated diagnoses, it is a terrible situation, and I could have ended up in that same predicament before.

And with the disorder, I must worry about being able to access my medication every day until my death. The risk and liability are not good. These books are therapy for that part of myself, the aspect of myself that roams the imagination.

I went from one point in my life while guessing my direction towards what I sensed to be truth existing somewhere to the present which was previously inconceivable. At 18, I was super normal whereas now I would say I am normal.

I must remind myself of what it was like to even feel that human as I had before. I was not as incredibly fractured as I am now. Though in matters of the complicated and existential, I have found my relationship with the Divine through the winding modes of my feelings and experiences at various moments.

The overall connection to reality is the constant link and is only pulled into awareness by your conscious and most humble effort. You cannot drag the ideological up to the heavens where ideology is absent. In the highest reasoning of heavenly realms, nothing is privatized or exclusive because all came from source. Your garbage does not even belong to you. Neither does the knowledge you come forward to observe.

It is mutual that you are worth nothing, because I am worth nothing. In a perspective of realized potential, we each believe the other is worth something, contrary to the existentially meaningless. To create a moment, idea, or anything, is our God-given ability. The Divine decorated the theatre stage with us as models of performative willpower.

We are on-stage right now, watched by the hidden existence. What will we do when we walk to the stage? Will we make a final break away from the expected and become free agents of our own light? The pressure of expectation on a situation tends to mutate the situation with biases. In the following subsequent events, consider our original biases going into the situation. Our biases are the masks we place onto our faces to disguise our true egos. We are going toward the future faceless, our original face will snap back on when we realize we have no control over anything.

I have searched for truth throughout my life in my own mode of curious nature. I had always been smart and, perhaps, some people would say above average.

I would have developed an ego for that, but as I have said up to this point, all of that was taken away from me by the force of a deterministic Nature. I was forced to give up my previous identity. I was to develop severe mental illness after 18 years old. This new identity is not shaped with the image I hold of myself. My identity is shaped by my experiences, from my subjective experiences. I cannot really say where my life would have gone had I not developed a mental disorder which runs in the genetics of my family.

I make a lot of comparisons in my mind to calculate the difference between two events or ideas. I see the need to show the difference between what led me from normal to abnormal. I must tell you who or what murdered my ego before I am taken away from your awareness as the author following the last page of this book. If I point to the difference made in my life and explain it further, I should be able to show you how to come across and make the difference in yourself.

How do you make it to Heaven?

You do this by perspective and perception. This state of mind is the state in which your awareness comes from the light of Heaven.

From the light you are looking from Heaven's realm toward your worldly existence in perspective, rather than looking up to it from your perspective as it is in this life. The eyes from Heaven see with compassion, acute insight, and understanding. Heaven is the moral regard. It is the upper emotional sphere we are to dwell in to reach toward contentment, passivity, and, eventually, enlightenment. When we exist in this state of being, we choose the good over evil naturally.

We were especially our best at points in our history, but the leading powers have decided for us. The decision was to reject the good for the bad. We are slowly giving into contempt, hatred, and other negative feelings that happen in similar nature to feeling lust. It's a subtle burning in someone, energizing them to make a hasty change toward aggression and isolation.

With each engagement in which we adopt another negative perception, we begin descending planes of reality because we personally envision a future for negative consequences. Every murderer shows a history and path leading up to the murder, a psycho-pathic climax. This also works vice versa with creating positive conditions. Every visionary follows a testimony leading up to the vision.

I have followed the calling in my life and simply wish to share the vision we all can have. Becoming alive to the perception that we sit in the fields of the divine, from a deified land that has source in heavenly ambitions.

People wonder how to reach enlightenment. It is a mystery, yet people have epiphanies and do not question their nature. To have an epiphany is to momentarily be guided directly from a higher perspective that immediately wins you newer knowledge and increased awareness of the present moment. It creates a spasm of thoughts which occur quickly and lead to a jump in thought patterns and self-realization.

You win the moment by aligning with the universal divine. You will be gifted with yet another clue on how we are supposed to think and view situations in our life. Jumping to new levels of perception guides us toward heightened awareness. People have mystical gifts. I know three people personally so far in my life whom all have the gift of premonitions in dreams. I mentioned one toward the beginning of this book, and how his premonition came true to my life.

We are informed by dreams in the natural state. When there is an allowed harmony between the unconscious and conscious, the two intermingle into a sublime reality to perceive. We are to better perceive this divine reality to discover evidence in the objective to further ascend states of being and reach divine union with existence. Or instead of going up, you can most definitely go down. That is the choice, whether to become a part of your enemies or not, even in the circumstance your foe is larger than you.

The ghost reality is the imagining of an afterlife. The secondary narrative to reality is decided by your personal language with the internal monologue. The Divine sits above our thoughts and dreams in the supreme reality as the ascended state for all creation. This is where art, nature, intelligence, and vision, all exist from one source in the highest state of perfection.

To think and to dream, those are personal inquiries among the presence of a collective vision. You can be guided by the willpower invested in your soul (psyche) equipped with an invigorated power of spirit. The spirit within ourselves as our perseverance is the energy maintaining the created state of self. It takes energy to be yourself. Spirit is the vehicle for conscious awareness. We exist within boundaries of Spirit though we retain the ability to do many things. It is with awareness that you are gifted the ability to truly control your mind and guide your chosen actions in a determined, willed, and mindful execution.

The greater good follows the cataclysms of all evil. The declination in the state of nature toward increasing chaos can only exceed for a temporary duration until the path is found for Divine Nature to succeed. The moral consists of two hatreds coming together to destroy and suffer great loss followed by the resolution of coming into one love. In this realm of time, the puzzle is *how long until you love everyone?* And you have a lot of learning to do, as we all do.

To solve this puzzle, we must discover the perfect consequence as an event in collective social reality. Following a global cataclysm, a massive act of love and compassion will appear that leads to negotiations and peace pacts forming between the lands of the world.

At present, we are fixed in a reality where we will suffer for as long as we want until the time comes where all of us in the world are pacified by our submission into the state of harmony which is the polarized form of chaos. In the state of harmony, which is an ascended state of nature, all events and things come together in perfect timing. Life begins animating as if it were a movie of the mind, a ride of our collective imagination. Life perceived as a collective dream has its positives in that anything may happen.

The Apocalypse is a collective event revealing the obscured and hidden dimension to our reality. This covert face of reality becomes sensible as we encounter a discovery of divine insight and meaning to create new context surrounding the world and life. Enlightening the world with a new light of reasoning which will captivate our knowledge and transform each part of the world into a haven for us to have prosperity. We will be made into a home planet.

We are of Spirit, and we certainly exist with the potential to live at the scale of the universe. The Apocalypse will remove the veil that I discussed earlier in the book, a veil of unknowing. What must occur to trigger the event is a massive collective realization that breaks the traditional sense for reality, an observation that shakes the world. This develops as a slow progression, and the steady burn of realizing a great truth will continue to accelerate further in time to completion. Upon approaching the door of eternal death is the ignition of spirit to express and become participative.

Therefore, we must seek the truth and continue thinking and allowing a free society where academics and philosophers are acknowledged. One where scientists and mechanics build the human future. I see the future looking as if a science fiction movie but with a postmodern form of spirituality present in narrative which is a transcended form beyond organized religion. We continue to live human lives but are equipped to know when the divine is communicating within us. We will only survive in the condition that we move forward as a strictly secular world civilization.

Divine knowledge is known through its specific nature and way of information. It is eloquent and coherent, and structures basic information in absolute expression, in ways that are identifiable and competent. Divine knowledge is information in the state of perfection and mastery, able to deliver an undeniable truth because it's compatible with all proven understanding and incompatible with false information. It stands apart and you will know it is significant.

The magic of the universe and Creation, what we understand as God, is not found in religion. Religion is an organized belief system that is established to aid your spiritual development, but we are quickly coming to understand it should not be represented in human governments to structure and organize the world. As nobody can represent the potential of spirituality better than another, because nobody can possess the specific inner potential of another. We are only possessed by a hidden potential from divine intervention, the emerging grip of the divine choosing you to fulfill a discourse while you are progressively informed going forward.

Are you chosen by the universe? Not at this exact moment, when this book has been written, but trust me you will be chosen if you are on the side of the world surviving the unforeseen calamities of tomorrow. It may not be now, but a different now as you read this later. You are chosen to know better because you can, and you will use the knowledge for the advantage of a higher divine agenda in the creative universe.

Mark befriended aeonic beings, spirits that have lived for a length of time that is not easily captured by our sense of time. These beings have no dependency on nature, they exist without oxygen and sustenance. They have knowledge that cannot be comprehended by many. In my schizophrenic imagination, there were eons which came together in creation to deliver passages of time to this universe. The aeonic spirit Harmony being one. This directly alludes to the previous-something universe I have spoken of previously, when everything came together in synchronized action creating a natural flow to reality.

This universe exists with the foundation of consequential reality. The consequential reality divided into spiritual, physical, mental, and social. When karma is present, it means there exists a disharmony in Nature. Karma developed a stratum of knowledge in good and evil.

The universe explodes with an expressive force to create and materialize. Then, it runs meaningless and regresses back into Source, the all-natural singularity. Once deprived of meaning and lacking the significance necessary to improve condition, the universe withers away becoming absent of meaning. It then gains new meaning once more by reverting back to its inner source of intelligence to discover more, with each chapter ending to set up the following chapter.

What makes this universe creative? The fact you have the right hemisphere of your brain as the creative half of mind. The development between logic and creativity is evolving the character of the universe. We will discover the obscured supernatural elements of our given circumstance once the mystical becomes logical. How we achieve that observation will persuade us away from the ultimate destruction. People will become paranoid from their heightened awareness, feeling as if being watched by the skies.

There will be an intervention between the confused world and the Divine. This is when the two *truly* begin to connect. We will become stricken and feel numb at the point we sense the presence of the Divine. We will stop sensing for this world only once at the realized presence of divinity. The world will be acknowledged, and feel acknowledged, by the Divine Universe.

Where does the light lead? As said before, it leads to the world of spirit. In the light is unlimited possibility. And that is why you may make another life possible, to later engage the light with more knowledge to better understand infinity. You will encounter an unlimited and infinite-reaching light founded in profound truth and experienced in incredible euphoria. The purpose of this light at the center of creation is to enlighten and revive you with new spirit so that you may continue to endure an eternity.

The human creation is extended away from higher reality by its descent into the realm of suffering. The Divine exists in a realm of light. Light is characterized by reasoning, truth, and harmony. We lack any formal reasoning for reality, and we understand this because of our present circumstance that expresses nihilism. There is no reasoning in life, this is evident because there is no obvious purpose. We exist in the shadow of light but above the Hell we believe to be eternal torment. The Earth dimension we all coexist within is an upper echelon of Hell, as it is a dimension of suffering. Hell is the source of anguish, deception, and confusion. The Earth dimension has these three qualities in a lesser degree, but they are present in our reality.

If we were to be one step above the dimension of suffering, we would exist in a dimension of euphoria, though that euphoria would not exist nearby to its highest level. Euphoria is the opposite of suffering. The lesser euphoric existence is a lower echelon of Heaven. In this dimension, there is inspiration, hope, and love. All knowledge present in this dimension is guided by those three principles.

At the contrary end of the euphoric echelons is our present dimension of suffering. Knowledge in Hellish echelons of existence is guided by negatives, those that I described as anguish, deception, and confusion. The Earth dimension is at the intermediate level between Hell and Heaven. We will continue existing at this lesser dimension of suffering for as long we remain hindered away from completing moral goods.

Knowledge exists at a potential to be deceiving or enlightening, and each of those two inherent qualities are engaged by your chosen state of mind, which is your perspective and default for perception. At a basic understanding, a good mood can bring in positive thoughts and a bad mood can bring in the opposite. The altered states of mind are characterized by having a complexity of self-involvement.

For myself, am I involved in perception as Dillon or Mark? I perceive as Mark and benefit from Dillon's experience. Ego loss is not a foreign feeling or uncomfortable for me as I simply adapt into fully being Mark. It's as simple as taking off the shoes that I wear in this life. In a general acknowledgment, I have a good personality, showing a sense of humor and compassion that brings relief to other people.

My life was typical until the age of 19 years old. At that point I descended downward to the Abyss of my imagination and its potential. My sense of self was defaced by being forced to consider the otherworldly and finer details of reality. I have come face-to-face with the afterlife, which I perceived in the medium of my imagination and its extension into my personal subjective reality.

The realm of thought is the mental plane expressed by the Spirit. And you can change realms within your mind by your subconscious effort. Our expressive thought is the unconscious mind given perceivable dimension. My thoughts conveyed to consider the otherworldly had brought a new shade of existence into my perception of reality. The hidden reality existing in the interiors of deep mind, the unconscious – what has not been expressed yet in the perceivable.

At an early age, around the time I was 14 years old, I struggled with fear of the afterlife. I could not decide which was more intimidating: the idea of eternal life or eternal death. To exist forever scared me, it scared me much more than to never exist again. That is a part of the reason I turned to atheism. To not believe in anything after death resolved my fear and phobia of existing forever in eternity. This was my safety in mind. Letting go of this life felt better than letting go of this suffering. And this is where the world has gone the wrong direction.

It feels good to demand grief from others while believing you are inherently excused by a universe that you perceive as supporting yourself. It is a high that we do not speak of and is one of extreme confusion that provokes hysteria. It remains a confused state because it is not properly informed as we do not know if the universe (or God) supports our words and actions. Living as if you are affirmed by God makes your cynicism feel like power. I have been far more existential in the root of personal growth; my fear of eternal life did not pertain to the concerns of the religious world.

What broke me of that fear was my descent into my imagination with the light of realization as my lantern. I understood it is not Earth forever and it is not now that exists forever. What exists forever is inspiration and possibility toward a more enlightened state of existence in the universe. The state of existence exists beyond the physical, into immaterial reality of mind, then toward the immersive light which stands before you. As it is at the end of reality, you will never go beyond. You will stay safe until you are prepared to meet the Divine.

The higher agenda is to open reality to the Divine. Whereas the evil that lurks in the world seeks to close reality from the Divine. You are here to find the balance so to set your feet firmly on top of the dead ground, for one day to capture the meaning you sought after for so long. The meaning you were meant to live for exists at greater depth than you could have ever imagined. To capture that meaning would indicate you have understood divinity. It all began non-physical, and it all will end non-physical.

From birth we are exalted by Spirit and continue with inclinations of the good to understand one day why it is good. It promises that you will be happy one day. If that very deep desire for happiness dissolves, you are more likely to die of Sudden Adult Death Syndrome.

One day when you have understood your adopted parent as the Universe, you will be told where to find your real father. He packed his belongings and went to God. When he believed he had found Heaven, he witnessed God to have an unfamiliar face and unfriendly demeanor, then your father fell dimension. There he found the Divine present in the only love found in lower dimension, which had taken him later to Heaven. This second venture into Heaven was different as it was nothing like his previous experience, it was completely transformed and unfamiliar. He found contentment in this Heaven.

It is not God that you think you know, because that God does not exist. The Universe exists, and so does the Divine. The two will lay you to rest one day and breathe life into your mind with Spirit once more. Your home is here all around you. Within a momentary lapse of suffering, you discover subtle comfort as the grace of the Divine Universe.

To be surrounded by an eternal good, or an eternal evil? You make friends with both sides for as long as you choose to identify with either. Though with a compassionate heart, you will continue to be sad knowing that everyone is caught in-between the good and evil. You must understand that the security in the Universe is not promised to anyone, and it is threatened. There is a possibility that demons will descend from the sky and the possibility they will not.

It is because of this possibility that the Divine finds our universe threatening. The armies of Heaven are now prepared and so are the armies of anti-Abyss. There is a force greater than destruction, there is a force that wishes to uncreate our existence and radicalize it to something far worse. You ought to realize how fragile a good universe really is and why you should never take it for granted or turn away. This is a part of seeking truth...

Truth is not black and white, simply there to conclude who is right and who is wrong. Truth may be presented within behavior, communication, and Nature. Truth is not a weapon to oppress, dissatisfy or punish. It is the opposite of a weapon, it is disarming. Truth is present to liberate, encourage, and provide for others. Truth is also a neutral force and incorporates balance in the presentation of Karma. The good guys can do mutual harm to the bad guys.

Therefore, good, and bad do not exist in a dualism that is effortless to discern.

The potential that is shared between two sides of a conflict is the regression of reasoning. Without the virtue of reason, our behavior degrades into senseless impulsivity. The consequence is we fall to deadly desires.

I was never told by a voice, and I was never shown a picture. I was informed by the emergence of a source for information in the potential of my mind. I attribute this *source* as being an inner gateway of the mind that expresses divine information and reasoning. I learned a great deal of knowledge and had been informed of something that matters far more than the global debate about the existence of God.

There are no words. No words to express the wretched state of our world right now. The Divine intention for creation has been disgraced on enough occasions in our history. So rather than learning from a history that cycles, we look to the Divine instead. The value of divine inspiration is our promise of something better. Find the truth and seek it. The divine truth will hold irrefutable meaning, and this is how you identify it. An unconditional truth. Information without an equal rebuttal, wisdom that enlightens, and realizations that cause you to reevaluate. This is seeking truth to provide ourselves more time in mercy.

Conform to natural laws of nature, becoming aware to the divine inner nature between self and all else. Transcend away from harmful anti-human theory and sentiments. Look at your impact, which should guide your reasoning with your willpower. Do not go radical over something because the perspective makes sense, you are changing yourself to make sense of it. What impact does that have? Think of consequence. This reality is a consequential reality. We are here to face the consequences of our actions and performative willpower. This occurs on an individual and collective level.

There is no longer anything to worship here. This is dead land. The Divine has left to the Sun to be away and slip back to allow for more possibility. Possibility is the mutation of potential circumstances happening. Experiencing possibility allows us a greater height to expand our awareness.

The loose phrasing in my attempt to quantify God is because in the grand scheme of things, specific worry about God does not matter. You were taught these things are of immense value and that is the deception. There is way more to realize than what has been captured by your mind and awareness.

If you walked the streets of Heaven in the non-physical environment of the City of David, would you wonder where the light from above is coming from or would you pay no mind? That is the question. Will you ever know the source of creation as your Creator? Or will you continue to worship idols of God? Nothing but your self can grant you the choice to seek more.

We knew forever the pain would stop after being physically punished. We knew forever the anger would reside after forgetting it. We knew forever the love meant something though it was not always there. And now, we both know the world is one of lies and the skies beyond are of truths. Though you are tired now, just know you will continue to endure as you scale toward the irrational Heavens.

When the social fabric of society all breaks down, it will all be in its rawest form. At that point we will not focus on all that is broken, but instead how we are going to rebuild it all. The journey to complete resolution is followed by undefinable ecstasy. It will be worth all the effort because finding that harmony will happen when we all seek truth. We lose the temporary upon the loss of blood. We will win the eternal upon securing the establishment of compassion in existential permanence and relevance.

We are here to protect harmony and chaos for the eternal heavens. This is performed by a resilient neutral effort that justifies both causation and its consequence with equal reasoning. This form of law disables the evolution of chaos and invokes accountability in life and its participation with the universe.

That is the purpose for humankind. There is only improvement once we have renounced the desire to excuse our wrongdoings and instead choose to rectify them. And to reform our collective behavior for the positive, we are destined to advance socially, discern truth, learn to reason, and discover our own benevolence. Take care on your journey in seeking truth, friend.

Enjoyed the book? Please support the author
and consider posting a review or rating online.

ABOUT THE AUTHOR

Dillon Jepsen was born in Bradenton, FL in the United States in November 1992. He grew up in his hometown throughout his life and went to college at Florida State University where he received a Bachelor of Science in Sociology. He works professionally as a funeral director guiding families through their experience of loss and grief. He also involves himself in acting and electronic music production. He is the author of the previous title A State of Mind.

Printed in Great Britain
by Amazon

29737773R00109